The Magician's Son

Sandy McCutcheon was born in New Zealand and has travelled and worked all over the world. He has been a theatre actor and director and has written plays, novels, children's books and works of non-fiction. He moved to Australia in the 1970s and currently lives in Brisbane, where he is the presenter and producer of Radio National's *Australia Talks Back* and *Australia Talks Books*.

ALSO BY SANDY McCUTCHEON

In Wolf's Clothing
Delicate Indecencies
Safe Haven
Peace Crimes
The Poison Tree
Blik
The Haha Man

SANDY McCUTCHEON

The Magician's Son

VIKING
an imprint of
PENGUIN BOOKS

VIKING

Published by the Penguin Group
Penguin Group (Australia)
250 Camberwell Road, Camberwell, Victoria 3124, Australia
(a division of Pearson Australia Group Pty Ltd)
Penguin Group (USA) Inc.
375 Hudson Street, New York, New York 10014, USA
Penguin Group (Canada)
90 Eglinton Avenue East, Suite 700, Toronto, ON M4Y 2Y3, Canada
(a division of Pearson Penguin Canada Inc.)
Penguin Books Ltd
80 Strand, London WC2R 0RL, England
Penguin Ireland
25 St Stephen's Green, Dublin 2, Ireland
(a division of Penguin Books Ltd)
Penguin Books India Pvt Ltd
11 Community Centre, Panchsheel Park, New Delhi – 110 017, India
Penguin Group (NZ)
Cnr Airborne and Rosedale Roads, Albany, Auckland, New Zealand
(a division of Pearson New Zealand Ltd)
Penguin Books (South Africa) (Pty) Ltd
24 Sturdee Avenue, Rosebank, Johannesburg 2196, South Africa

Penguin Books Ltd, Registered Offices: 80 Strand, London, WC2R 0RL, England

First published by Penguin Group (Australia), a division of Pearson Australia Group Pty Ltd, 2005

10 9 8 7 6 5 4 3 2 1

Text copyright © Sandy McCutcheon 2005

The moral right of the author has been asserted

All rights reserved. Without limiting the rights under copyright reserved above, no part of this publication may be reproduced, stored in or introduced into a retrieval system, or transmitted, in any form or by any means (electronic, mechanical, photocopying, recording or otherwise), without the prior written permission of both the copyright owner and the above publisher of this book.

Design by Cathy Larsen © Penguin Group (Australia)
Typeset in 12.5/18pt Granjon by Post Pre-press Group, Brisbane
Printed and bound in Australia by McPherson's Printing Group, Maryborough, Victoria

National Library of Australia
Cataloguing-in-Publication data:

    McCutcheon, Sandy.
    The magician's son: a search for identity.
    ISBN 0 670 04210 2.
    1. McCutcheon, Sandy. 2. Adoptees – New Zealand – Biography. 3. Identity (Psychology). I. Title.

362.7340993

www.penguin.com.au

For my children
Guy, Cathryn, Alia, Maha and Yvonnne

*Those who are bent by the wind
shall rise again when the wind softens*
										Te Whiti

Contents

Introduction	1
Part One	5
Part Two	169
Postscript	291
Afterword *by Bronwen Watson*	305
Acknowledgements	311

Introduction

This is the story of a search for identity. The tale of a small boy who was not only taken from his family but told that his family never existed. A boy brought up to believe that his residual memory of his real parents, and even his own name, were figments of his over-fertile imagination. In effect, that his deep-seated physical memory was a lie.

The contradiction between what I was told as a child and what I believed took me on a journey, half real, half fantasy, that lasted for almost fifty years. One of the literary heroes of my teenage years, Isaac Bashevis Singer, once observed, 'No doubt the world is entirely an imaginary world, but it is only once removed from the true world.' In my search the two melded, leaving me often suspended between truth and fiction. I took some comfort in the fact that Singer also said,

'When I was a little boy they called me a liar, but now that I am grown up they call me a writer.'

Writing this story has been one of the hardest things I have ever undertaken. By comparison, writing novels, children's stories, and even plays, was a breeze. Most people experience an understandable discomfort when writing about themselves; self-revelation is an awkward business, especially if, like me, you harbour a strong sense of self-doubt. It is a job for the dedicated narcissist, not someone who instinctively avoids mirrors.

My attempt to track down the truth about my adoption has been both painful and confusing. Painful because it raised issues that decency and commonsense would suggest were better left untouched. (How, for example, to write about the unhappiness at the heart of a child who'd spent his life denying an overwhelming sense of abandonment and the constant fear of rejection, who'd succeeded in distracting himself from even contemplating those emotions? A child whose escape into fantasy was so accomplished that truth and reality had little meaning?) And confusing because I was extremely adept at not only creating and wrapping myself in a cocoon of whimsy, but also wiping huge tracts of childhood memory from my mind. Whether my selective amnesia is due to the trauma of being taken from my family at an age when I would have known and recognised them, or to damage sustained in an early experience of physical violence, I will never know.

Bringing my few childhood memories to the surface was a

gradual process that took place over many years. Sometimes a fragment would arise unbidden, vanishing as quickly as it had come. At other times, usually when I was deep in the throes of a writing binge, a window would open onto my subconscious and out of nowhere would come a flood of memories. Things that had long lain buried came back in an unsettling rush. I owe a profound debt to my muse.

There were moral questions too that had to be addressed. How ought I write about the family that adopted me? On the one hand they enabled the life that I have – they provided the education, the childhood home and the material stability. Yet they also hid from me the facts of my adoption, and when I did discover that I was adopted they lied to me about it. These were people I loved and whose love I craved. They were also people from whom I became estranged because of my behaviour. There's no escaping the fact that I was a difficult and troubled child; I plunged too easily into a world of fantasy and I hurt those who, in their own imperfect ways, were doing the best they could. If I were a magician I would conjure up the dead and say that I am sorry.

And how to write about the dusty old skeletons that I discovered in other people's closets? Was it right to expose them to the light of day? Would it matter to anyone now living that one of their ancestors had been born on the wrong side of the blanket, or had secret vices? Would I upset or offend my newfound family?

In the end I decided that the search was for *my* truth, and that whatever I uncovered along the road to that truth could legitimately be revealed. There were just two cases, however, where I felt that some people would be unduly saddened by certain chapters of the family story, and I have quietly closed that particular closet and left the skeletons in the dark. Mind you, any amateur gardener glancing at my family tree will quickly identify some rather shoddy graft work, but I leave that and the pruning to others.

In digging up the past, I have uncovered an incomplete record. A jigsaw puzzle with many pieces missing. There are some pieces whose shape and place are ambiguous, but I have discarded none of these. There are other pieces which at first appeared to be deeply rooted in fact but which turned out to be fictions of my own creating. Other, fictitious-seeming pieces, once dusted and examined, emerged as solid fact. A few linger, shimmering in the half-light between worlds. I let them all remain.

Part One

Chapter 1

'You're a little Nazi bastard,' Ian said to me.

Ian was in my class at school. He was a tubby kid with what I have always remembered as a streak of cruelty. How fair this is I can't say, but over the years I've thought of him as one of the bad guys. Reflecting on it now, I see that I actually owe him a lot. Without him I might never have embarked on the journey that followed.

I have no clear recollection of the circumstances of Ian's announcement. I don't even remember where he said it or why. But it was sufficient to move the tectonic plates of my being, and in the aftershocks that followed, the details were swept away. There are moments that change things. This was one of them. I was nine years old.

Ian's tone had been matter-of-fact. He was simply telling

me something that he believed, rather than being vindictive. Nevertheless his revelation took a while to sink in. There were a couple of new words to check out for a start. At nine I had no idea what 'Nazi' or 'bastard' meant, although it didn't take me long to find out. Of course I asked my parents about Ian's comment, but they dismissed it out of hand. The notion that I was adopted was, they told me, 'ridiculous'.

It took me another few weeks to pluck up the courage to ask Ian's parents. Here, too, I can not recall the exact conversation, but they did confirm that I was adopted. I also remember them making a reference to my mother being a Red Cross nurse during World War II, and to the thousands of children whose parents didn't survive the war. Many of these were still in displaced-persons camps, I was told, and a large number had been sent to New Zealand from orphanages all over Europe and Britain.

Years later, when I happened to mention Ian's name to friends in New Zealand, they asked me if I was aware that he too had been adopted. I wasn't. But maybe this explains why he felt strongly enough to make an issue of my situation.

As for his parents, I've often wondered why they chose to be so honest with me. Perhaps they had thought through the impact of adoption on a child more than the McCutcheons had. Or maybe Ian was himself one of the children displaced by the war in Europe. Whatever the reason, it's impossible to underestimate the difference their revelation made to my life. I shudder at the thought that they could so easily have lied to me too.

The remarkable thing about that unpleasant moment in the schoolyard is that for almost three decades it stood as my very first distinct memory. My recollection of anything before that was shadowy, full of shapes and wraiths, real and imagined. From time to time some more vivid memory would rise, but often it was received memory – things told me by others, which I appropriated and claimed as my own. My early memory was a quicksand within a maze. There were no signposts, no markers, and few islands of stability.

Having no early memories and no real trust in the future, I grew up living very much in the moment, hanging onto the present as the only reality. Here and now I was safe. Before was dark and dangerous; the future was uncertain.

More strangely, I thought that the way my memory operated was normal, that this was what most people experienced. When I heard people reminiscing about their early childhood I considered them either extraordinary or delusional. It was only when I began to look for my past that I realised it was I who was the exception.

I was not a happy child, yet even now I can't say for certain that I was conscious of the reasons for my unhappiness. The indicator of my state of mind was my behaviour. I was, as one adult later reported to me, 'a troubled child'. I was disruptive, quick to anger; I craved attention. All for no good reason, my adoptive parents told me time and again. They frequently – and accurately – pointed to the fact that I had been given everything and yet still I was unsatisfied. Ungrateful, they called me.

The conscious mind of my pre-nine-year-old self is a vast, empty canvas on which, over the years, others have painted. A paint-by-numbers exercise that still has great unfilled areas:

'You must remember . . .?'

No, but now that you've told me, I'll remember you did so.

The bulk of my early memory is acquired, not actual. It's not real, and it's therefore unreliable. Sometimes clues arrive out of the blue. A rare and very welcome proof that I wasn't always a difficult child came from an old classmate, John White, in 2000. He had read one of my novels and decided to track me down.

> On a November day in 1955 a freckled-faced, ginger-headed little fellow showed me a great kindness which I had forgotten until picking up a book (*Delicate Indecencies*) at Sydney Airport. I was leaving Ilam Primary with my family, bound for the UK, and this classmate presented me with a gift for the journey, wrapped as I recall in the torn-out page of an exercise book and containing a compass, protractor and set square. In

hindsight great navigational tools. I am not sure if I communicated it at the time but it was a very touching gesture.

If memory is like a filing system, then my system is odd, to say the least. It is highly selective. Personal items might well have been filed, but retrieving them can be nigh on impossible. However, I can remember with absolute clarity facts I learned in history at school. On my first visit to Sarajevo I was able to walk directly to the spot on Franz Joseph Street where Gavrilo Princip assassinated Archduke Ferdinand and the Archduchess Sophie of Hohenberg. Even obscure facts remain clear: since the age of thirteen or fourteen I've had no trouble remembering that Leonardo da Vinci invented scissors, that Al Capone's business card stated he was a second-hand furniture dealer, and that Winston Churchill was purportedly born in the ladies' room during a dance.

Yet ask me the date of my first marriage and I have to sit down and figure it out. I have never been able to trust dates. Until recently, events to which most people attach great importance – births, deaths, life-changing moments – existed without the date stamp. It was as though my own past were a no-go zone, a foreign country for which I'd not been issued a visa.

Interviewing people in my professional work has led me to believe that even a healthy, normal memory can at times be a sideshow mirror, one that does not so much reflect reality as distort it. The reasons for this are as varied as each individual: to pander to vanity, to absolve guilt, to preserve a suitably sanitised form of the past... Early memories can be particularly unreliable. The magical realms of one child's fantasy world are as real in memory as the dark reaches of hell another might have inhabited. But the traumatised child uses survival strategies that can make their memories more unreliable than most: suppression, denial, obliteration. I was an expert in all three, yet for a long time was oblivious to my skill and the reasons for it.

Freud would probably have considered me a textbook case of his 'pleasure principle' in action. His theories on memory seem to be more about forgetting; indeed his most interesting observations on the subject are contained in a book entitled *The Psychical Mechanism of Forgetfulness*. If it is not pleasurable, Freud believes, we drive it out, drive it down, hopefully erase it. The good doctor holds that our unpleasant experiences are forced out of the conscious mind deep into the subconscious, where they remain out of the reach of memory.

The habit of suppression, once acquired, is addictive. I learned the mechanism early and oiled it with practice; it's something that has accompanied me from childhood to the present. I am not arguing the case for memory loss here, rather for a well-trained memory – one trained in the art of suppression. We all stand in front of mirrors of our own choosing.

Yet an intact memory is vitally important to the creation of a sense of self. Cut off from memory, we would be rudderless. With no semantic memory, we would be nameless. Without episodic memory, we would respond to everything as if discovering it for the first time. Life would be a nightmare. Daniel Schacter, Chair of Psychology at Harvard University, claims in his book *Searching for Memory* that memory is critical in providing 'the underpinning for our whole sense of self, to allow us to tie together all the different moments in time that comprise a life and somehow to make sense of that, to pull it together in a way that gives us a feeling of existing not just in the here and now but existing in time as a person with a past who can look forward to the future'.

I grew up in a disconnected no-man's land; I grew up not believing who I was. This was, in the early years, based on nothing concrete. There was no tangible thing I could point to, but rather a feeling that the Old French word *desaise* comes close to capturing: a lack of ease. Close enough, too, to *disease*: something buried deep and working its way through my system. In the process of finding my past I also found the cause of my lack of ease, and ultimately the cure. In the final stages of the journey more and more memories came flooding back. It was a perplexing experience to be an adult experiencing childhood memories for the first time.

When I was an infant everyone called me Sandy. I certainly looked like one. Pale skin, red hair, freckles – I had all the attributes. Yet although I learned to answer to the name, I was never comfortable with it. It felt like an ill-fitting skin, one that needed to be shed. Still, with use, it moulded itself around me.

I had other names too: Robert Hamish McCutcheon. My real names, so I was told. But who was this Robert Hamish? Certainly nobody ever called me Robert. When I was older I grew to like the name, but by then it was too late. Nobody ever called me Hamish either.

My friends all seemed to fit their names. John looked like a John. David looked like a David. Philippa looked like a Philippa even when she was called Pip. For her the diminutive worked. But Sandy? It was a diminutive of none of my names.

To search for ghosts is difficult enough at the best of times. In the classic version of the ghost story there's a house with a reputation for being haunted, giving the story a locale, a physical reality. But the ghosts in my story had all been cast out; they were homeless, hungry ghosts who left no trail. As a child I was constantly being taught to forget: Forget your old name, you are now called Sandy. Forget, and in return we will give you everything. But after forgetting who you are, you will remember who you have become, who *we* say you are. You are a McCutcheon. Never forget that. There's a place for everything and everything must be in its place. And you, of all people, should know your place.

So I am taught. But I don't believe any of it and my sole option is to rebel. Rebellion is the only way I have of validating my existence. I act out deep-seated emotions without being able to intellectually grasp why.

I know from talking to people who knew me as a young child that I evinced a desperate need to fit in. The language used to describe me then is diplomatic: nervous, talkative, annoying, frenetic, attention-seeking. I plead guilty to all of the above. I was attention-seeking because I needed attention. I needed someone to listen to what ailed me. But I didn't know what that was myself.

The story of my search for my real identity is not straightforward; the fragmentary nature of my memory mitigates against any logical retelling. When I write that I remember a certain event happening before the age of nine, this is a memory I have retrieved in recent years, or have been told by someone else, not one that I've carried with me since the event's occurrence.

Even my date of birth has been an uncertain anchor. For many years I was unsure whether it was a real date or one created because the bureaucratic machine demanded I have a number. My birth certificate shows the date 17 February 1947 but gives no indication that I have any parents. I first saw this certificate just before I turned eighteen, but I'd been consciously questioning my date of birth, along with my name, from the moment Ian let the cat out of the bag that I was a little Nazi bastard.

It turned out to be a rather feral cat.

Chapter 2

The McCutcheon family were established and 'comfortable'. A neat family: two adults, two children. Mary and Mac, Sandy and Mary Jane. As nuclear as you could get. More importantly, it was a family from the right side of the tracks – a Fendalton family. Fendalton is a middle-class Christchurch suburb with style, class, perfectly kept gardens and a lot of old money.

On weekends the McCutcheon family would travel to one of our holiday houses – Akaroa in summer, Arthurs Pass in winter. If we stayed at home in Fendalton, it would be lawn-mowing and car-cleaning on Saturday, and mid-morning church on Sunday. Sunday lunch was invariably a traditional roast that had cooked while the family – minus Mac, who always stayed at home – was at church. During lunch my father would put a record on the gramophone and we would listen to classical music. It was all very normal in a privileged kind of way – at least on the outside.

Hugh Maitland McCutcheon – known as Mac – was a dentist. He was a big, solid man, with close-shaven hair that always reminded me of the German generals in war movies. Mary Eva McCutcheon was a short, slim woman with an attractive face. The two of them had all of life's necessities with a fair few extras thrown in. Their marriage seemed very happy and I can't recall a cross word between them. They had plenty of cross words for me, but not for each other.

My sister Mary Jane, a couple of years younger than me, was always a 'good child'. She was cute, quick-thinking, well balanced. I suspect she was also shy, or maybe she only seemed so in comparison to a brother who was noisy, needy, and so insecure he was constantly seeking attention. Mary Jane was everything I was not, and more than once I was told I should be more like her. But although I was incapable of emulating her behaviour, our parents treated us equally well. On birthdays and at Christmas we always knew we could look forward to presents that were interesting and well suited to our needs and wants.

It wasn't until the 1990s that I discovered Mary Jane had also been adopted. By then our relationship was so strained that I'd seen her only a handful of times in some thirty years, but it still struck me as extraordinary that her adoption wasn't something that appeared to concern her greatly. Or if it did she never admitted as much to me. When we finally talked about it, in the year before Mary McCutcheon died, I learnt that my sister knew her mother's name and where she lived. The fact that she had this information – the very thing I had been craving all my life – and yet had never wanted to make contact was inexplicable to me.

How and when Mary Jane came to learn of her adoption, who told her, and at what age she came to live with the McCutcheons are things I've never been able to find out. All I remember is that as I was growing up she was always there. In retrospect it seems that her ability to accept her adoption without question might have made it hard for her to understand why I could not, and why I found it almost impossible to deal with the not knowing.

As a child I was very quick to fit in socially, and as a result I enjoyed our outings with other families – as long as I didn't 'forget who I was'. This was my weak spot. But most of the time when we went out as a family we were a well-drilled unit. Neat and tidy. Polite. Our manners were as groomed as our hair, as polished as our shoes. It didn't take me long to learn that it was best not to 'muck up' in public. Any infringement I did commit would not be mentioned until we got home – there was never any airing of dirty laundry in public – and the usual punishment was being sent to my room on a duck's diet: water only.

Our first family home, in Roa Road, seemed large, as all childhood houses appear large. Going back years later to look at it, I found that not only had it shrunk but the land had been subdivided, and there were now two houses instead of one. I have always hated losing homes and I was upset when we moved from our quiet little street to Fendalton Road. I was ten or eleven at the time, and having to abandon our old home caused me much sadness.

The house in Roa Road was extremely neat, with everything in its place and everything in moderation. The living room had a beautiful piano at its centre. The armchairs all had antimacassars, even though no male member of the McCutcheon household in living memory had ever put Macassar oil on their hair; the faintest whiff of Bay Rum was the limit, and that only after a visit to the barber. (They were barbers then, not hairdressers.)

Out in the back garden was a rotary tilting clothesline – not a Hill's Hoist but an original McCutcheon design, one of my grandfather's inventions. It proudly bore the McCutcheon name in raised letters on the winding mechanism. I've often wondered why my grandfather didn't become rich from selling the patent. At the rear was Mary's favourite tree, a small Judas tree (*Cercis siliquastrum*), with tiny pink flowers around its heart-shaped leaves. It must have been stunted, for I grew faster than it did and I don't recall it ever reaching beyond a metre. Maybe my parents were secretly eating it; I read somewhere that the pods and flowers are edible and quite tasty fried up in fritters.

Mary was responsible for the ritual quality of much of our life. Yet although she was always busy, I can find no record of what else she did with her days. She had her golf, and certainly she looked after us. For many years she had a domestic help, Mrs Parsons. Par-par, as we called her, remains in my mind as a figure of sweet comfort, baking, cleaning, and always ready with a 'blue bag' to dab on bee stings. She is surrounded in my memory by the smell of apple pie with cloves, and hot scones. We would spend hours together in the kitchen top-and-tailing gooseberries, the comforting warmth of her large thighs beside me.

Mrs Parsons returned to me many years later as a character in a children's book I wrote. I borrowed what I remembered of her and placed her in a role in which she would have felt at home – looking after a motherless boy. When an audio version of the book came out I didn't bother to listen to it until a young boy was visiting my house. As we listened together and I heard my words come back to me courtesy of a professional actor, I realised just how much a figure of comfort and love Mrs Parsons had been. When my sister or I needed affection Par-par was there. Our parents must have appreciated how much she gave us, because when she finally retired Mac bought her a small house in the neighbouring suburb of Riccarton. I remember missing her very much.

By evening Mrs Parsons would be gone, and it was Mary who was ready with gin-and-tonics when Mac got home.

They would sit in the living room and have a drink together, music playing quietly. Later there was television, but nobody in our family seemed overly impressed with it and it's my impression that we watched very little.

Mary's character was much like her physique, wiry and tough. She was extremely well spoken and a stickler for detail, truth and a tidy house. She had been trained as a nurse, but beyond that I knew little about her past until her funeral, when I discovered that she had received several awards for bravery during World War II. One of the stories recounted at her wake was of her days as a nursing sister on Crete, where she stayed to nurse the wounded even as German paratroopers were descending. Ordered to leave on the last boat, she nearly blew herself up destroying a truck that would have otherwise fallen into enemy hands. Between Crete and Alexandria, Mary was on at least two ships that were sunk before she made it safely to shore.

As a child I once came across a photo of her atop a camel. I asked her about it and was told it was nothing important. Looking back, it's difficult to tell whether her reticence to talk about herself was unusual or not. She was of a generation for whom talking about oneself was considered bad manners.

Mary had another attribute which, with hindsight, seems anomalous: she was a dedicated smoker. Whereas Mac might have a cigar on New Year's Eve, Mary always had a packet of Rothmans cigarettes with her. When as a teenager I was castigated for smoking I retorted that if it was okay for Mary to smoke, then why not me? Mary defended herself with the claim that she was a Rothmans shareholder and was supporting her investment. It was the only indication I ever had that she owned shares. She and Mac did have property investments but the size and extent of them was never discussed in front of us children.

Mary McCutcheon's family were Crawfords, and her father had been a sailing-ship captain and a harbour master at the Christchurch port of Lyttelton. I have no memory of there being much talk about the Crawford family, but Mary had a brother who was a doctor or medic in the war in the Pacific. I only discovered this during my teenage years, when I invited the daughter of a Japanese industrialist home for dinner. It was as though I had tossed a grenade into the house. Mary went white and left the room. Mac pulled me abruptly into the kitchen.

'Get that girl out of the house,' he said to me. 'Now.' His tone brooked no discussion. He handed me some money and suggested I take her out to a restaurant. Later he told me that Mary's brother had been executed in cold blood by the Japanese. My attempts to extract further details about this were curtailed with the comment that it was 'something we don't talk about'.

There were, as far as I'm aware, only two Crawford cousins, Garth and Ewan, but I have few recollections of seeing them during the time we were growing up. Although they lived in Christchurch, I don't remember them visiting the McCutcheon home, nor did they ever go with us to Akaroa or Arthurs Pass. I later got to know Ewan quite well when he was working as a ferryboat captain in the North Island town of Tauranga. He and I shared a passion for *The Goon Show* – I once spent an absolute fortune on an eight-track tape recorder in order to feed my obsession. The little I know about Garth I learnt from Mary McCutcheon's letters to me decades later. He became a farmer and Mary appeared to have been fond of him; she would often mention him, although she wrote nothing of Ewan.

Mac McCutcheon was an only child and there seems to have been no other relatives on that side of the family, apart from his parents. My memories of his father, like so many others, had always been hazy. The last time I saw him alive I was probably eight or nine, but decades later, when I was living and writing in Finland, a profusion of memories of him resurfaced. This was, to say the least, a strange and unsettling event.

Late one night, while I was sitting by the fire, he appeared to me – not in the flesh but on the page. I was living in a cottage in the Finnish forest and I had positioned my writing desk close enough to the fire for warmth while still preserving my view of a landscape blanketed by snow and bathed in moonlight. As I was writing, my grandfather McCutcheon came suddenly to mind. I jotted down the few things I remembered about him and as I did so other memories flooded in.

I had always regarded my grandfather with great fondness, and I had a moment of intense pleasure remembering the sound of his voice, and that his eyes were brown, and that it was not he but his house which had the musty smell that I have ever since thought of as the smell of old age. My grandfather used to live in a damp old house in Dunedin (several hours' drive from Christchurch), and as a child, I now recalled, I had a sense of it being if not haunted, at least impregnated with other people's memories. Old music stuck to the ceilings like cigar smoke. There were odours of strange food and gas cookers. Somewhere was his wife and talk of a wasting sickness. Rooms were locked away from children, and everywhere were the smells and shadows of private history – the smell of Grandfather McCutcheon.

I remembered that I had always thought of it as his house, for his wife was really only present in the form of a yellowed photograph on the piano. Mostly she was ill in bed, but she must have come out occasionally because I had vague recollections of hearing her play the piano. I felt that if she ever moved about that house it would have been on tiptoes, as though she too were a visitor, afraid to disturb the shadows in the halls or the dust on the stairs. As she drifted silently towards death she became more like her photograph; she started to yellow and grew so insubstantial it was as if she were already gone.

The saddest thing about these memories of my grandmother was that I only remembered that I had once remembered them. They were like echoes of a memory rather than memories themselves, for she had never been strongly present to me even when she was alive.

My grandfather, though, had been much more real, and suddenly his name too, until then quite forgotten, came back to me: William, known as Bill. I recalled that he'd had a special bed, a magic bed it seemed to me as a child. Whenever I visited the Dunedin house it would appear, and when I left it would vanish again until I returned. The bed was in the wall of the study, in an upright position behind huge oak doors. The mattress was held in place by the girth of some enormous horse, and once the bed was lowered from the cupboard, my grandfather and I would struggle to unstrap it. My fingers were too small and weak to free the buckles, and as my grandfather grew older his fingers would tremble with the strain. There might have come a day when he was too old and I still too young to unharness the bed, and yet we would still have found joy in opening the doors and lowering it into place. I was secretly afraid that when I slept in the bed it would return to the cupboard with me in it, and I would find myself trapped inside the secrets and shadows of the house.

I had other vivid memories that night by the fire: of my grandfather carving notches in the rim of a cotton reel, making a toy for a sandy-headed young boy who would go through life trying to recall how such toys were made. A cotton reel, a rubber band, a matchstick – did the stub of a candle come into it somewhere? The reel became a toy tank, inching its way across the faded linoleum of a Dunedin kitchen floor, grandfather and boy on their knees, enthralled.

These images of my grandfather were so intensely real to me that I found myself having an imaginary conversation with him, saying things I'd never given voice to.

'I went to your funeral, Grandpa.'

He looked up. Did I really use to call him that, or was it Granddad or Grandfather?

'Was it a good funeral?'

I shrugged. 'My father couldn't go. I think he was ill at the time. They said I had to represent him. "Be the man of the family," my mother told me.'

'How was that for you?'

'Scary. Especially when they said I had to go and look at you. I didn't want to, but they insisted.'

'How did I look?'

'Dead.'

'I expect so.'

Then I suddenly remembered the Finnish connection. On one of our family visits to Dunedin my grandfather slipped a small Finnish knife – a *puukko* – into my hand. As I drew the birch-handled blade from the reindeer-skin scabbard, I saw the word 'Suomi' etched into the metal.

'It means Finland,' my grandfather explained. Reaching over, he took the scabbard and pointed to the leather tassels. 'When they move they keep away the evil spirits.'

I was entranced. He then produced another gift, a beautifully carved wooden sleigh and reindeer joined with real leather traces.

'It's also from Finland,' he said. 'Lapland, the land of the Lapps.' In the driver's hands was a small but detailed whip.

Were my grandfather's gifts the genesis of my love affair with Finland? The reason I was drawn to learn the language, live in the country?

Then I recalled that the knife and the sleigh had not been my first encounter with Suomi. Mac had had a skiing friend called Arne Sandelin. His thick Finnish accent, along with the smell of tar and ski-wax, would seep through the dark into my bedroom in the alps. Many nights I would lie in the dark listening to the adults talking of history, talking of pain. Implanting new places and events in the mind of a boy who should have been sleeping. The civil war, the Winter War, Germans, Lapps and Russians, Reds and Whites.

But now my grandfather was smiling at me. 'Tell me about my funeral.'

'They'd put you in a box with shiny handles.'

This time he did not look up.

'They put a wreath on top of the box. Then the box slid through a hole at the end of the chapel. I couldn't see any flames. I should have been able to see them. After a while, when people were crying, blowing their noses and shaking hands, I went around the back to have a look. But you were gone. All that remained was the box with the handles and the wreath. For years I wondered how they burnt you without damaging the beautiful box.

'I didn't go to my father's funeral, Grandpa,' I went on cautiously, expecting a reproach.

Slowly he turned his head back to the fire and rubbed a gnarled hand over the grey stubble on his jaw. The shadowed part of his face was blue. 'He didn't come to mine either.'

'He couldn't.'

'Still . . .'

'They didn't want me to go to Mac's funeral. I was in disgrace at the time.'

The flood of memories receded and I took a moment to store them carefully away, making sure they would never be lost again. They felt even more precious for having come back to me in the cottage in the Finnish forest, a place I'm sure my grandfather McCutcheon would have loved. When he died I lost access to his mysterious house in Dunedin, and when my father died in the 1970s, hard and unforgiving, I lost the small cottage at Arthurs Pass. I always intended to become rich one day and buy it back.

In 1953 a series of events began that set me on a course towards a career in the arts. In December of that year the SS *Gothic* berthed in Auckland harbour and the usually staid New Zealand population went crazy. This was the first visit to the Land of the Long White Cloud by a reigning British monarch. I was six years old at the time and the behaviour in my own town was no less bizarre: farmers dyed their sheep red, white and blue, and the same colours adorned almost every public building in Christchurch.

According to family legend, Royal Tour fever had infected the McCutcheon household several months earlier with the arrival of a telegram from Buckingham Palace. Early on in his life, Mac McCutcheon had been a talented violinist who, if the stories are true, was one of the first New Zealanders to win a scholarship to England's Royal Academy of Music. During his stay he performed at Buckingham Palace for King George and his family. The young Elizabeth had particularly enjoyed his music and so, before setting out on her coronation tour of the colonies, she had a telegram sent requesting that Mac play for her. The arrival of this telegram was the signal for a frantic bout of activity. Mac retrieved his violin case from the rafters of the garage where it had been gathering dust and began a hectic rehearsal period.

Looking through the records of the royal itinerary for that visit, it is difficult to tell if he ever gave his performance. Maybe it occurred at a civic reception or a garden party. But myth or fact, it doesn't matter. Though I was not particularly moved by the presence on our shores of Her Majesty – who was described by the *Auckland Star* as an 'orchid under cellophane' as she travelled through the city in a bubble-topped limousine – my father's violin playing had a profound effect on me. How a man with such huge hands could elicit such sweetness from a fiddle still amazes me. My own visits to his surgery had left me in no doubt that he lacked the digital dexterity to perform as a dentist.

The events surrounding the royal visit are all received memories, the source of them probably Mary McCutcheon. My only actual memory is of a feeling of disbelief that anyone with the talent Mac displayed could have left his violin in the rafters of the garage for so long. It is possible that he'd played the violin at home before this time, and I have the sequence of events wrong, but what's most relevant is that I was deeply impressed by his virtuosity.

My admiration grew even more when I discovered that some of his performances had been recorded on old 78 rpm records. Even during the unhappiest times in my childhood, when I stormed and ranted against my father, I never stopped loving his music, and to this day I can not listen to a piece of Gemiani or Mendelssohn without thinking of the music that seeped through the walls of the house in Roa Road.

Why had a man with such an obvious talent and passion for the violin given it up to become a mediocre dentist? And how did someone with so much anger inside produce such beautiful music? Mac's story, pieced together from a variety of sources, has always struck me as a poignant example of how one incident can change a person's direction in life.

Mac McCutcheon had been studying music in the United Kingdom when World War II broke out, and rather than return to New Zealand to join the fighting, he and his friends immediately volunteered for service in the RAF Bomber Command. As history was to show, it was an extraordinarily dangerous service to be in, and if the Kiwi boys had any illusions about what lay ahead of them, these were soon dispelled. Between September 1939 and August 1945 almost one million tons of bombs were dropped, some nine thousand aircraft were lost, and 55 573 men died. Very few of the Kiwis made it home alive.

Mac, however, had been rejected due to colour-blindness, and disturbed by the deaths of his friends, he returned to New Zealand. He tried again to enlist, but instead of a combat role he was given the job of entertaining the troops by playing jazz fiddle. Not one to fiddle while his friends were being killed, he put the violin away and managed to qualify as a dentist. It was only the telegram from the Queen that drew the violin out again. Had this not occurred, I feel certain it would have remained gathering dust in the garage. I mean to thank her, if I ever get the chance.

The discovery that my father had this wonderful artistic

side had a huge impact on me. Perhaps, I reasoned, since I had always felt like an outsider in the family, an intruder – unwelcome at times, at others a disruptive annoyance – if I could appeal to my father's creative nature, I might find the acceptance and approval I so craved. That music moved my father and me in exactly the same way was undeniable, and no matter how estranged we became, I clung to the belief that if I could only connect with his artistic side I would be accepted.

My musical abilities proved to be limited, but I remained convinced that Mac would respond positively to my acting and writing. Yet he continued to be openly hostile on this front, and when I left school and embarked on a career as an actor, the family told me in no uncertain terms that I had wasted my education and let them down.

Chapter 3

The family mantra, 'a place for everything and everything in its place', was equally apt for Christchurch in the 1950s. It was the ultimate tidy town, and always had been.

One hundred years previously, the Canterbury Pilgrims had laid the city streets out with mathematical precision and built their homage to England. From Cathedral Square to the leafy suburbs of Fendalton and Merivale, a visitor could be forgiven for thinking they had been transported to an English city.

Private-school boys bicycled through the streets in blazers and straw caddies. Gowned varsity students took time off from study to punt down the River Avon, trailing their fingers in the crystal clear water, smoking languidly and watching the fat trout slip into the protective shade of giant weeping willows.

In winter the fog came down so low it hid the tops of the oaks and plane trees in Hagley Park, but in spring the park was transformed into a riot of daffodils and blossom. Walking from Fendalton through the park to the city in summer, you could smell roses on the air. Next to the park and abutting the heart of the city was one of the world's great botanical gardens, along with the museum, which was housed in a magnificent stone building that looked as though it had been shipped direct from Oxford University.

In the city streets the cars were all shiny and spotless. It would never do to take the car into town without cleaning and polishing it first. The occupants of the cars were just as pristine. Everyone seemed to wear tweed: suits for the men, skirts for the women. Their coats were expensive. The women wore what my mother referred to as sensible shoes. The men's footwear was as shiny as their cars. You should be able to see your face in your shoes, I was repeatedly told. The women had pearls and cashmere jumpers, the men gold, onyx or greenstone cufflinks and studs.

The only odd touch was the tweed hats the men wore; they looked like they belonged on the head of a crofter or a fly fisherman from the Shetlands. If you looked closely you could see that many did indeed sport a fishing fly hooked into the band.

When you entered the main department stores the staff all greeted you respectfully by name, their accents terribly British. You were known. You belonged. And just as the streets and the minds of the citizens were all 'shipshape and Bristol fashion', so too was the future. Presbyterians sent their daughters to Rangi Ruru Girls' School and their sons to St Andrew's College. Anglicans went to St Margaret's and Christ College. And the Catholics? Well, we didn't talk about them in my family. The financially less well off sent their children to Christchurch Boys' High or Girls' High, both fine schools.

Once a suitable school education had been completed, the debutante balls began. These marked the start of the mating ritual that brought together the children of the landed gentry and the Christchurch professionals. The North Canterbury farmer's daughter would marry the Christchurch doctor's son. There were rules and expectations in this society, albeit unwritten and unspoken ones, and the social order appeared very comfortable, ensconced in a sense of its own decency. All was neat. All was tidy.

Yet beneath the surface all was not so wholesome. Away from the beautiful gardens, behind the fine oak doors and brass fittings, festered some nasty interiors. Christchurch, suffering from its fixation with Englishness, was at heart oppressive and racist. In Christchurch white was not simply a colour.

On other fronts too all was not as it should be. A government inquiry in 1954 exposed a wave of 'shocking immorality' so 'lascivious' that it was deemed necessary for parents to be alerted. The inquiry's findings were released to the public and a copy of the quaintly titled 'Mazengarb Report on Moral Delinquency in Children and Adolescents' was distributed to every household in the country.

At first it seemed to the city's middle class that all bad things happened elsewhere. Christchurch might have had more Scottish pipe bands per head of population than any other city in the world, but in the less salubrious suburbs to the east the parties were getting louder. Dancing spilled out onto summer lawns, empty bottles onto the roads. Drunken youths hung out in parks. But then the infestation moved towards the heart of the city. In Cathedral Square motorbikes were parked untidily. There were men in leather jackets. Young women were smoking in the street.

A feeling of disdain towards these outsiders grew into aggression. Who did they think they were? And where on earth had they come from? These teddy boys who had suddenly appeared. The bodgies and widgies who were in town. I remember being told at the age of seven that nice people didn't hang around in milk bars, and because I knew my parents were afraid of them, I watched these so-called milk-bar cowboys with much interest.

Out in Fendalton things were still calm. There was no great moral panic. After all, the popular wisdom went, youth was just a passing phase. Ignore it and it would go away. The government knew what it was doing. The film censor had banned *The Wild One*, starring Marlon Brando, and *Rebel*

Without a Cause, with James Dean. But the wraiths were gathering. A new generation was slowly stripping away the genteel and fragile Englishness and revealing a neo-gothic nastiness and, in a strange way, the true nature of a city that should never have been built. The harboursides of Lyttelton had been too steep and dry for the early settlers, forcing them down to the swampy plain. Now the swamp was rising. And worse was to come: not just cracks in the facade, but beasts sucking at the very marrow of respectability.

Enter two pupils from Christchurch Girls' High: Juliet Hulme and Pauline Parker. Juliet came from the right side of the tracks. Juliet was one of the 'nice people'. She was the daughter of Hilda Hulme, a vice-president of the Marriage Guidance Council, and Dr Henry Hulme, the rector of Canterbury University College. They didn't live in Fendalton, but in some splendour in the nearby suburb of Ilam, where Juliet had gone to the same primary school I was currently at.

Pauline, on the other hand, came from very different stock. Honora Parker and Herbert Rieper, her parents, weren't actually married, although they had lived together for twenty-three years. Herbert managed a fish shop.

The world would probably never have heard of these girls if not for a chain of events set in motion by the good rector's unhappy little secret. He and his wife had a third person living in their home, an English engineer called Walter Perry.

When Juliet walked into her mother's bedroom and discovered her mother in bed with Walter, the family imploded. The university demanded Henry Hulme's resignation and divorce proceedings were instituted. Henry decided to send Juliet to live with an aunt in South Africa while he headed back to England.

This was too much for Pauline and Juliet. They were inseparable, and had other plans, one of which involved going to America and publishing the books they intended to write together. When Henry Hulme refused to include Pauline in his plans for Juliet, the girls turned to Pauline's mother. Honora Parker didn't hesitate. She turned them down flat.

Juliet was fifteen and Pauline sixteen when, on 22 June 1954, they lured Honora Parker up to Victoria Park in the Cashmere Hills above Christchurch. After a pleasant stroll along one of the paths through the park, they battered her to death with a half-brick inside a sock. Forty-five blows to the head. It took only a few minutes, but Christchurch was to reel for years.

The trial, with its underlying themes of insanity and lesbianism, shocked the city's homophobic and patriarchal society to its core. The case became a cautionary tale about the evils of lesbianism in young women. It also marked a dividing line between the generations. The disciplinarian attitudes of many adults were hardened in response to what they saw as dangerous tendencies in the young. Suddenly a frightening spectre of what independent teenagers were capable of was seared into adult consciousness. The post-war teenagers were a danger to themselves and to society. Secretly the teenagers wondered at the power the two girls had exerted.

It is arguable that the class divide also grew wider as a result of the murder. It was the middle class versus the working class, and mirrored the Cold War divide of West versus East. Those living in the west of the city – in the bland, elitist suburbs of Fendalton, Riccarton and Merivale – eyed those in the east with even more suspicion. Evil lurked in the east. Which was ironic given that Parker and Hulme hatched their murder in the western suburbs.

Because Juliet Hulme had been a pupil at Ilam Primary, exaggerated stories about the scandal circulated in the school playground. The stories grew with the telling and had little to do with the facts. In the McCutcheon household, on the other hand, the murder was never mentioned. For a few weeks the newspapers stopped being left around on the kitchen table, and for my sister and me life went on as before. Many adults considered the topic of the 'moider', as Pauline Parker had called it in her journal, taboo. It was best not to acknowledge it had ever happened. But no matter how deep the good folk of the Garden City buried themselves in their bridge, golf or tea parties, innocence had been lost. It was never to be regained.

Fendalton's Roa Road comes back to me as my first experience of community. Across the road lived the Meyra family: Wiff and Betty and their children Jane and Nicholas. They were close family friends, skiing folk. Jane was my age and someone I always felt great warmth towards.

Making contact again after almost forty years, Jane, whose childhood memory is flawless, recounted an episode from when we were about three years old. Mary McCutcheon and I were visiting at the Meyra house and I had acted up to such an extent that Mary shut me in Jane's room. This upset Jane, and she remembers asking her mother why Mary treated me so harshly, to which her mother replied that Mary did not know how to deal with me.

Our nextdoor neighbours on one side were the Dendles, a conservative family who lived in a two-storey house that overshadowed ours. One of their daughters I recall as being very cute, but it was Libby I was attracted to. I remember her because I was given a thrashing by my father when we were caught at about the age of five exploring the differences between boys and girls. 'Such a dirty thing to do!' my mother scolded. Fortunately the incident didn't affect my ongoing interest in that area of research.

On the other side of us lived an elderly couple, good Christchurch working-class folk. I remember nothing of her, but he was a house painter and I loved spending time in his garage watching him mix the colours together, surrounded by the heady smell of paint and turpentine. To this day I find the smell of turpentine incredibly evocative. The word itself trips back into my mouth, its syllables retreating.

Our neighbours over the back fence were, in contrast to the well-ordered McCutcheon household, refreshingly wild and chaotic, an unruly oasis in our regimented suburb. That is not to say we didn't have our own moments of chaos, but these were usually brought about by me.

From the age of four or five I had been telling anyone who asked me the ludicrous question, What are you going to be when you grow up? that I was going to be the *famous* McCutcheon. The first step towards that goal came when Mac bought a Bell and Howell camera and ventured into home movies. One in particular, 'The Roa Road Film', was quite an undertaking. My father must have spent weeks on the production, because the end result was a skilful take on the old silent pictures, complete with caption boards.

The scripted dialogue was as melodramatic as the overacting. I was cast as a 'wild child' and in one scene was required to stand in the sandpit and throw a stone at a window in the woodshed at the back of our garden. There was to be an action shot of me throwing, and the next shot would pan to the broken pane of glass. One of the window panes was already broken and due for replacement, and production costs were thereby kept at a minimum.

But my aim was off and I managed to score a direct hit on

the unbroken pane. If my father had been quick enough with the camera he might have captured a dramatic and shattering moment. He chose instead to get extremely angry. My acting career was terminated at that point and took some years to re-establish. It took even longer for my aim to improve.

A couple of years later, I became the proud owner of a beautiful archery set with metal-tipped arrows and a bow so strong I could hardly draw it back. One memorable day, I was playing with it in the grounds of Christchurch Boys High. The school was at the end of Roa Road, and a friend and I were playing some kind of game involving ducking out of the way of oncoming arrows. My friend's ducking was no better than my aim, and when he ran into an arrow just below eye point it was the end of my Robin Hood phase and of the friendship.

I was not much better with guns. My father owned a Diana air pistol that fired both lead slugs and lethal little darts, and I was allowed to practise with it. After the incidents with the stones and arrows, however, my target shooting was restricted to the weekends we were at Arthurs Pass. On rainy days I would spend hours thumping darts within reasonable proximity to a dartboard, but lead slugs and I were to have a rather extraordinary encounter a few years down the track.

I would have been fifteen or sixteen when I got shot. It was a beautiful Sunday afternoon and I had walked around to my friend Guy Hargreaves' house. From the gloom at the far end of the Hargreave's long dark hallway, Guy's brother called out in a faux-American accent, 'Eat lead, stranger!' There was a pop and I felt a sharp pain in my lip. Guy's brother stepped forward lowering an air rifle, the colour draining from his face.

I was so shocked that it took me a few seconds to realise what had happened. Blood was seeping from my mouth and lower lip. My tongue, prodding gently, came into contact with something hard and small rolling around my mouth. Shock aside, it was too good a moment to waste. I walked the length of the hall, spat what I thought was my tooth into my hand and offered it to him. 'There!' I said triumphantly. I glanced down and to my amazement saw a crushed lead slug. 'I caught it with my teeth,' I added hastily.

The aftermath was less dramatic. My lip, now bleeding profusely, proved to have a perfect hole through it. We hastily rang the nearest doctor and were informed by his protective wife that Sunday was his day off, so we made do with cotton-wool and a bandaid. The slug retained a perfect impression of the tooth it had struck and I kept that slug for years, marvelling at how close to disaster the moment had come. A few centimetres to the left and it could have hit me in the back of the throat. That might well have been more serious. I've lost the slug now, but I still have the tooth.

Another old McCutcheon home-movie clip shows a party in the backyard at Roa Road. It looks like a lot of fun. A freckle-faced boy is laughing and showing off, not quite the centre of attention he wants to be. He is awkwardly out of harmony. Outside of grace. Close to people but never swept up and embraced. But in another film I can be seen skating on Lake Pearson in the Southern Alps, and on either side of me, holding my hands, are Mac and Mary McCutcheon.

As a child I loved going to the movies, and my routine on those weekends we were in town was established early. Once I was considered safe on a bicycle, it was off to the barber on a Saturday and then to the Riccarton movie house to see the latest episode of *Hopalong Cassidy*. All these years later I have no trouble recalling that the actor who played Hopalong was William Boyd and his horse was called Topper, and for sixty minutes on Saturdays I would ride with them as they righted wrongs and overcame evil.

My own acting career began in an unconventional way at Ilam Primary School when I was six or seven. The setting was a school excursion. The teacher had instructed the class to visit the toilet before boarding the bus. I was in such a state of excitement – a bus trip into the city to the museum! – that of course I didn't go to the toilet, and I was fine until we reached the ancient-history section of the museum. But when you've already told the teacher you've been when you haven't, you can't ask to be excused, so I drew upon the skills of improvising that I was already developing and which were to stand me in good stead all my life.

My eyes alighted on a large model of the sphinx, and whipping around behind it I quickly relieved myself against its hind leg. Then, without being spotted, I rejoined the class just in time to witness the teacher and my classmates standing transfixed by the sight of a golden stream spreading slowly from the rear of the sphinx. The Miracle of the Pissing Sphinx was such a convincing performance – I never was identified as the culprit – that I was hooked.

Chapter 4

It was in the McCutcheon family's holiday homes, away from the strictures of life in the city, that I did most of my growing up, most of my pushing of the boundaries.

The summer holidays were spent at Akaroa, and I was usually in disgrace for 'forgetting who I was' – that favourite line of my mother's. This was generally a result of my having discovered something new. It was in Akaroa that I learnt how easy it was to get drunk on Bacardi, what a cigar tasted like, how to steal sweets from shops, and how awkward it was to get your hand up someone's knickers in the back row of the Gaiety Theatre, even when they tried to help.

In Akaroa's bush-covered Domain, at the not so tender age of twelve, I worked out the mechanics of copulation with a doctor's daughter. Despite her father's profession, she had no more practical knowledge of the matter than I. The hot days, steep banks and nettles mitigated against any romantic mystery, but we returned weekend after weekend to practise. We never improved. The whispered secrets of sex were a powerful incentive, yet all I managed to achieve was a rash on the knees. In the end we gave up and concentrated on learning to smoke the cigarettes she stole from her father. At this we were an unbounded success.

When I was very young we had a simple holiday house at Akaroa. Mac and Mary later sold this and purchased a larger house in Watson Street, where my father installed a small dental surgery in the basement and began seeing a few patients on weekends. This house became Mary's full-time residence in the years following Mac's death in 1972.

Returning to Akaroa in in 1995 after a long absence, I found the place greatly changed. The sleepy sense of community that I remembered had been replaced with an entrepreneurial zeal. The town was now a popular tourist destination, with fine dining and luxury accommodation. It was still a beautiful spot, but the houses and the people were different. The old weatherboard and plasterboard seaside baches, as they were known locally, had been expensively renovated and now nestled into their tidy gardens with an air of dignified complacency. In one coffee-and-cake cottage (you no longer found Devonshire tea) the boule court was in play. It could have been a scene from the south of France. I felt decidedly ill at ease.

Regardless of this, everything about Akaroa brought back childhood memories – yachting, and getting wrecked on the rocks when I was caught by a southerly buster; waterskiing behind the family boat, which was named *Mary Jane II* after my sister; pulling up crayfish pots with my father in the swirling kelp beds out near the heads. I used to love those deep, green waters and at the same time I feared them. Kelp fronds splayed out like the arms and hands of the drowned, reaching for me. Stingrays floated among them like giant malevolent butterflies.

Whereas the deepwater bays down towards the towering heads that marked the harbour's entrance were morning places, the mudflats were reserved for the long summer evenings. Just before dusk we would move to the shallows in search of sole and flounder, feeding the net out in a long slow arc from the stern of the dinghy. The whole family would join together to pull it in, my father and sister on one rope, my mother and me on the other.

'Slow down!' Dad would yell. 'Keep it even.' Keeping things even has always been a problem for me.

The last time I was in Akaroa, in the winter of 1999, I felt a sudden pang of regret as I strolled around the town that our boat was no longer moored just off the beach. I longed to be able to row out to it in our dinghy, unclip the covers, prime and start the outboard, unhook the chain from the buoy and motor out on the misty waters. Off the beach was the raft where I'd swum countless times. It had been moored there for as long as I could remember, and every summer saw it crowded with kids diving and bombing into the beautiful clear waters of the harbour. At this time of year its only visitors were gulls. Further along was the little wooden jetty with the gazebo at the end, where as teenagers we would gather to share a cigarette, or a bottle of beer that someone had swiped from their parents' fridge.

I turned off the main street and strode quickly along the jetty, watching the coruscations made on the water by a weak sun breaking through the clouds. It had no power to warm. I looked along the beach and had a sudden memory of years before.

Every summer in Akaroa a Christian revivalist group would hold rallies on the main beach. We kids would all beg to attend because, apart from an excuse to get out of the house, there were free lollies. Standing in neat rows, we'd perform the actions to the songs we were taught and wait for the moment the lollies were flung into the air. Having remembered that much, I was powerless to stop a tune entering my head, and then, more irritatingly, the words returned: 'I may never march in the infantry, shoot with the artillery, ride with the cavalry. I may never fly o'er the enemy, but I'm in the Lord's army . . .'

No doubt I'd sung along willingly enough and performed the actions with alacrity, but it all seemed so militaristic now, and it galled me that such memories should claim space in my head while important ones remained elusive.

The gazebo now seemed dirty and had an unpleasant smell of urine. I retraced my steps back along the jetty, buffeted by a wind strong enough to chill me to the bone but not strong enough to wipe out the feeling that I was a stranger here. There had been so many changes since I had first come to Akaroa, and I resented them. The town had moved on in what seemed like an easy transition, whereas I was stumbling through my life.

Self-pity was pretty disgusting, I castigated myself, and just as I was deciding to redirect myself to more positive thoughts, I found myself outside the shop on the corner opposite the beautiful old post office. The street was full of ghosts and memories. I crossed the road to relive a moment from years before, one that had never left me. Finding the exact spot, I stood on the eerily deserted street and played the movie in my head.

Over the years, Akaroa had had bad luck with hotels. In 1882 three of them, The Grand, The Bruce and The Criterion, were burnt to the ground in one night. The arsonists had prepared well, gathering dried gorse and stacking it up against the back walls of each hotel and setting it alight. Three hotels in the neighbouring bays had also burnt down the previous week. The fires, it was soon discovered, had been set by temperance extremists.

53

In the early 1960s my close friend Tony Slyfield had been due to check into Akaroa's Metropole Hotel. When the news arrived that the building was on fire I raced down the hill and watched in horror as it burned out of control. In the confusion there was no way of finding out whether Tony had checked in the previous night or not, and so I stood helplessly by, along with most of the town's small population, as the shabby old Metropole was destroyed. Faces were illuminated by the flames, painted red, flushed with the heat; we squinted into the maelstrom, knowing that death was present but not knowing whose.

The following day, the searchers found several bodies – blackened, unrecognisable mummies – but not Tony's. He arrived the following afternoon, unaware of my concern, delayed by a fate that was cruelly keeping him for its own scheduled appointment.

Not long after his return to Christchurch, he was the victim of a senseless accident. Someone had stolen a warning light from a roadworks site and Tony, driving at night, hit a 44-gallon drum. A piece of the timber barrier rail flipped into the air and came down through the car's windscreen, killing him instantly. It was one of several deaths of people I knew during my adolescent years, but without doubt the one that affected me most.

The McCutcheon family's second holiday house, at Arthurs Pass, was two-and-a-half hours' drive from Christchurch, in the heart of New Zealand's Southern Alps. In the 1850s European settlers exploring the high tussock country at the foot of the alps were told by the Maori about a pass they used for bringing *pounamu* (greenstone) back from the West Coast. In 1864 the pass was surveyed, and with the discovery of gold on the West Coast a road was hurriedly constructed during the particularly cold winter of 1865. It was a road I was to travel hundreds of times. And so many of the trips were the same...

My mother would hand me a carton of food and tell me to help Mary Jane pack the car. Outside, the August morning would be still and cold under a clear sky, my father's breath forming clouds as he checked the oil and water in the Rover. His Arthurs Pass attire was invariably a tweed cap and thick, Aran-style jumper. His trousers, as ever, were baggy.

'Just put that box on the drive,' he might say, and he'd be grinning at this point. 'There's supposed to be snow on the road and I need to check the chains.'

I'd smile back, glad of his agreeable temper but ever wary of his notorious mood swings.

Snow on the road was a good thing. It meant a greater chance we'd be able to ski. It also meant that somewhere en route we would have to stop and put the snow chains on. That was fine by me. I had become quite adept at laying out the chains, even in the dark. Often we needed them to get to the top of Porters Pass, which signalled the halfway point of the journey and the beginning of the mountain roads. At other times we would get all the way to Arthurs Pass only to find we had to put the chains on to travel the final few yards to the house.

Having checked the chains, Mac would stow his two half-gallon bottles of draught beer, known to one and all as 'pigs'. Satisfied that all was in order, he'd lower the boot and gently push it shut. He'd take a cloth and rub away a small spot. Mac loved Rovers so much that during the 1950s and '60s he bought a new one every couple of years, working his way up through the models until he purchased a Rover 2000. The only one I have a clear memory of was the Rover 90 in which I learned to drive. The trip to Arthurs Pass took in a variety of road surfaces, from ice to gravel, and proved great training; with one exception I drove for the next forty years without accident or incident.

Every time we set out for Arthurs Pass there was a change in the family atmosphere. The tension seemed to diminish with every mile we put between ourselves and Christchurch. My father's jaw would relax and his eyes would sparkle. Mary cracked jokes and her language became less formal. It was as though the family were stifled in the city, all of us doing the things that were expected of us rather than those we craved. Akaroa was closer, the journey there taking only an hour-and-a-half, and we never quite managed to leave the pressure of the city behind before we got there.

The road to Arthurs Pass headed due west from Christchurch, up the imperceptible incline of the Canterbury Plains and through the towns of Darfield, Sheffield and Springfield. The farms on either side of the road were boxed in by macrocarpa windbreaks, the trees fused together into giant hedges. Their tops had been given immaculate crew cuts that resembled my father's. Along with the spectacular sight it afforded of the mountains getting ever closer, the trip was a window onto a much wider world – the natural world, where people were not always in control.

I came to know that journey like the back of my hand, but no matter how many times I travelled it I never failed to be struck by it. The history associated with this road fired my imagination more than anything I ever learned at school. Sitting in the back of the car, I was fed the stuff of legends, and of future novels – the raw material for a life as a storyteller. Sometimes I would count the milestones and imagine making the journey in a Cobb and Co coach. There were tales of goldminers frozen to death; of valleys where people had been lost for ever, their bodies never recovered; of small shacks where eccentric characters had lived lives shrouded in mystery. There were mountains that were referred to as killers. The stuff of childhood fantasies.

Just short of the point where the Torlesse Range signals the beginning of the mountains, we'd come to Sheffield.

'Ice-cream time,' I'd say hopefully from the back seat, glancing at my sister for support. But Mary Jane would stare steadfastly at the mountains and maintain a diplomatic silence. She'd been down this road before and knew where it led.

'I don't think we need an ice-cream in this weather,' my mother would reply, and my father, anticipating my next move, would catch my eye in the rear-view mirror and shake his head. 'We can all have an Eskimo Pie up at the store,' he'd promise, meaning the shop at Arthurs Pass. Mac liked ice-cream as much as I did.

Right on cue my mother would chip in. 'Last century a man named Robert Colthart used to live near here. He imported the first tennis racquet and tennis balls in Canterbury. Way back in the 1880s. Imagine that.'

Stupid. If he'd imported two racquets he could have had a game with someone.

The last little township before we'd reach the mountains proper was Springfield, the birthplace of one of my heroes, Rewi Alley. I must have been about fourteen or fifteen when his name was first mentioned on one of our car trips to the pass. My mother was talking to Mary Jane about the women's suffrage movement in New Zealand, and as we drove through Springfield she commented that Clara Alley, a leader of the struggle, had come from the town.

'Mother of the notorious Rewi,' Mac added.

'I don't think we want to talk about him, dear.' There

was something in my mother's voice that made me think, Oh, yes we do. Let's talk about him!

'Who was he?' I asked.

'Not a very nice man.'

I knew better than to pursue the matter, but I stored the name away for later retrieval. There wasn't much about Rewi Alley in my school library, but the main public library in Christchurch gave me more. Rewi was born in 1897 and had gone to school at Christchurch Boys' High, where a frustrated maths teacher told him that the only thing he'd ever be good for was breaking stones. Rewi is reported to have replied that if breaking stones was what was required, then such an ability would be an asset.

The more I read about Rewi, the more I liked him. In 1916, lying about his age, he enlisted in the army and went to war. He returned twice wounded and with an award for bravery. After working for a time as a farmer in the North Island, he happened to read a report on the 'Yellow Peril' and in 1927 announced to his family that he was going to China. It was intended to be a short trip but Rewi remained there for the rest of his life. He was committed to the communist revolution and to raising the education standards of the Chinese, and was given a job as a school headmaster. Surviving assassination attempts by the nationalist Guomindang, he went on to become a friend of Chairman Mao, Edgar Snow, Che Guevara and Fidel Castro.

For me, a restless teenager during the turbulent 1960s, Rewi Alley was an ideal role model. Not surprisingly my parents saw him as a traitor, so it's ironic that it was from Mac McCutcheon that I first heard the expression 'gung-ho'. This famous Chinese communist slogan, meaning 'work together', was Anglicised by Rewi Alley, although I'm certain Mac had no idea of its origin. Nor, apparently, does the Oxford dictionary, which attributes its adoption into the English language to the US marines in 1942.

Climbing up out of Springfield, the road would begin to wind into Porters Pass. When its 945 metres were dressed in pure white it was time to put the chains on, and Mac would look for a suitably flat section of road to stop.

He and I were a team when it came to snow chains. As soon as he tipped them out of their sack I'd pounce on one and lay it behind a rear wheel. Mac would lay his out, inspect mine, and with a nod of approval get back in the car. I'd stand in the biting wind and signal the moment he'd reversed neatly into the middle of each chain. Crouching in the snow, I'd pull the chains over the tyres and force shut the link locks on the now freezing metal. I always hoped Mac would trust me enough not to check. But he always checked.

On the slow drive up Porters Pass the snow would blow in flurries off the mountain, and the cars heading down had snow on their roofs. This section of the road was steep and twisting, and we'd grind our way up in low gear. If a lot of cars had gone this way before us we'd slot into their tracks and make it smoothly to the top, where we'd stop and let the motor cool down. The snow would whip off the ground around us and stream past, creating an unnerving sensation of movement. The sky was dark, the tops of the ranges buried in clay-coloured cloud.

Travelling on, we'd pass Lake Lyndon, where I learned to ice-skate, then Castle Hill, where huge trolls had been turned to stone: these magnificent limestone outcrops looked even larger when dressed in hats and trousers of snow. Then on to the lakes – Pearson, hourglass-shaped and beautiful, and the smaller Grassmere – whose surfaces were sometimes a mirror, sometimes grey speckled with the white of wind-whipped foam.

Some way further along, we'd cross the wide expanse of the Waimakariri River, whose headwaters either reflected a spectacular panorama of cloud-piercing peaks or were invisible in the gloom. Here the river flowed fast over boulders strewn along its snow-braided bed. When the snow built up on the car's windshield the wipers had trouble coping, and I'd be despatched, scrambling for my gloves, to clean it off.

And so to the cottage itself. The persistent image I hold of this from my early years is of ice on windows. Ice on the inside of windows. This was something I found on waking every morning, and I would spend hours studying the intricacies of the crystalline structures. At school we were taught that every snowflake was unique, but I didn't believe it. The

American photographer Wilson 'Snowflake' Bentley was the first to photograph a snow crystal, back in 1885, and he went on to collect some five thousand flakes, never finding two that were identical. But the number of flakes in just one decent-sized snowstorm was large enough to boggle the mind; that each should be different seemed impossible to me. And so I checked them – and I did the same with ice crystals.

I found the dendrite snowflakes fluttering down on their six crystal wings pretty special, and the patterns on the windows were just as complex. After examining them, I would melt the ice crystals so that they'd refreeze – I didn't want to have to look at the same pattern all day. With warm hands and breath I could create my own slow kaleidoscope.

This wasn't just about the physics of crystals, it was about obsession and security and stubbornness. I had evidently discovered at an early age – although I didn't conceptualise this until I was much older – that deep concentration on something stilled the turmoil in my mind. If I was engaged I was less needy of others. When I was absorbed in something the inner ghosts remained at a respectful distance. While not consciously doing so, I taught myself to contemplate whatever was in front of me.

Many years later, a Tibetan lama told me that this was akin to the Buddhist practice of 'being here now'. In a strange way I owe my ability to apply myself single-mindedly to any task to that childhood fascination with ice crystals.

Those early years at Arthurs Pass also stand out as the time I was closest to Mary Jane. In the cottage, which was called Woodsmoke, we'd lie in our separate bedrooms in the mornings and wait for Mac and Mary to call out that they were walking down to the general store. This was a long way for small feet and so I'd burrow under the eiderdown until the front door banged shut. Then I'd hear the noise of my sister's feet hitting the floor in her bunk room and I'd be up and racing her to our parents' bed – a large ocean of eiderdown under ice-framed windows. Had there been only one window we would have been fighting, but with two we each had our own. Wrapped in the quilt and propped up with pillows, we'd start on the ice.

We never touched the ice on the windows in our own bedrooms if Mac and Mary were in the house. One noisy scratch and Mary would know we were awake, and we'd be bundled out and ordered to get dressed. But with them gone we scratched away furiously until we had a hole large enough to peer through. The sun would be sending its first shafts over the high peaks, stealing the early pastels from the sky and exploding our ice-ringed portals with cold fire. Although the brilliance hurt our eyes, we stared out at the snow-covered railway station below us – and further, to the black hole of the tunnel entrance.

Arthurs Pass was a tiny railway settlement at the eastern entrance of the Otira tunnel, which burrowed through the mountains to the West Coast. To Mary Jane and me, the tunnel itself was a dare, a dangerous cavern that swallowed entire trains. Not the steam trains; for them, Arthurs Pass was the limit. From here to the coast the trains were electric, and yet mist and vapours issued from the tunnel mouth. If you stood close by you could hear it sigh. You knew it was dangerous inside. Maybe dragons lived there.

Once, the whole family walked through the tunnel to Otira, on a day when we were told that no trains would be running. It was damp and ferociously cold and every step of the way my heart was pounding, knowing they had lied about the trains. And nobody had mentioned the dragons, or rock falls either. Mary Jane and I both knew the story of the men who were trapped when the roof of the tunnel collapsed as it was being dug. Rescuers drilled a hole through to the workers, inserted a pipe, and poured soup down to them until they could be got out.

At our windows Mary Jane and I would listen for steam trains to come shuddering and skittering along the cold iron, fighting for traction in the frost, slipping on the icy rails down Bealey Gorge below the pass. The echo carried for miles on those crystal mornings and we were spurred on to clear a larger hole, big enough for a train to fit through.

Once the train was in view, we would dress and run down to meet it at the station, where the driver and the stoker hauled us up into the cab. There were metal plates in the cab, and wheels and knobs, and the dragon's mouth that ate the coal. It was a place of forbidden things – dirt, grease, steam, and oily rags that hung from the driver's pockets.

After the freight cars had been uncoupled, we rode to a turntable where we jumped down to help the shunters slowly swing the monster around. Then it was on past the signal tower, its arm at half-mast, to the water tower and the flapping canvas hose that fed the boiler with water to cool the dragon down.

Later, as my behaviour got more aberrant and Mary Jane was old enough to understand the effect this was having on the family, we grew distant, and eventually became estranged. When as an adult I learned of her adoption and came to envy her easy acceptance of it, I recalled that there were times as a child when I resented her. She was pretty, well behaved and academically bright – everything I was not. Yet we could have been allies. Together we could have presented a united front to our parents and demanded answers. But somewhere between those early years and puberty, Mary Jane sided, naturally enough, with my parents. This only increased my sense of isolation within the family, and more and more I took to doing things I could do alone: skiing, sailing and mountaineering.

In the absence of solid family relationships, homes and places came to assume great importance in my life. As did physical landscapes – I stored these inside and they became a surrogate home, a surrogate family that could never reject or abandon me. To this day I carry the imprints of those mountains at Arthurs Pass so deeply they feel like part of my genes. It's in the mountains that I relax, no matter where those mountains are. I have felt the same sense of belonging in places as diverse as Austria's Tyrol and Morocco's High Atlas. In some small way this helps me begin to understand indigenous peoples' links to their land as something far greater than real estate.

When I started writing novels I drew, often unconsciously at first, on settings in the Southern Alps. *Delicate Indecencies* includes a scene with a cinder path that crosses railway tracks, where a signal, rusted at half-mast and slowly tilting from years of neglect, stands like an uneasy sentinel. I was writing about Arthurs Pass, but it was only once the words were on paper that I realised where the images had come from.

When the protagonist in *Safe Haven* needs somewhere to retreat to in order to make sense of his problems, he comes to the mountains around Arthurs Pass. His moments of aloneness echo my youthful joy in that place. Unlike the claustrophobia of Christchurch or the numbing pleasantness of Akaroa, the alps provided me with space. Aloneness was possible there. You skied over a ridge and you were alone. Turned a bend in a mountain path and found nothing but a silent world of damp moss, gnarled trunks and wisps of old-man's beard.

Danger, too. Moments of heightened awareness as you roped up and began the breathtakingly cold passage across a swollen stream, with its slippery boulders and hidden depths. The intoxicating possibility of death. Rivers flooded, avalanches killed people. If you had an accident, there was no one to go and get help. Later I would come to know this same intense at-oneness with the moment through intense meditation.

And there was another danger that I discovered in the mountains: perfect beauty. It terrified me when I first saw it, and to this day the memory of it causes me to shudder.

As a teenager I set off one midnight to climb a mountain. At first light I was standing on a high peak in a dawn so cold that thinking was almost impossible. I was exhausted and exhilarated in equal measure. Before me the rocks were covered in blotches of pastel lichen – birthmarks fallen from the sky in colours of duck-egg blue and mescal pink. The colours of years of sunrises and sunsets. High above me stratus clouds were shredded by the brilliance of stars that burned brighter than my memory has been able to retain. Slowly the clouds were tinted sullen purple, then orange, and finally they became wisps of pink, strung in teased skeins between the peaks.

For several minutes I stood transfixed as the colours washed the icy face of the mountain opposite, which rose out of an ink-black valley still lost in the night below. Then the deep recesses of the valley gradually abandoned the chiaroscuro of ice and rock and bled through indigos and purples, reflecting the colours of the sky in a slow-motion replay.

It was a moment of such perfection that I was afraid there was nothing beyond it. While the ephemeral nature of perfect beauty might have escaped my teenage intellect, the image has remained with me ever since. It was one of three occasions in my life when I would have been content to die.

All my life I have chopped wood. Beech in New Zealand, stringybark in Tasmania, silver birch in Finland. Beside the cottage at Arthurs Pass, next to a large tussock, sat the chopping block and sawhorse. Beside them, patiently awaiting the saw and the axe, were the limbs of beech trees collected in summer. Out in the snow Mac and I would face each other across the sawhorse. His hands were large, his arms strong. Mine were puny and my fingers would feel the cold of the metal saw even through mittens. Inevitably my fingers would slip.

'Concentrate!' Mac would bellow. 'Get a grip!' When he got angry I got scared.

An hour would go by; my arms would be aching, my feet in the slushy snow would be numb with cold. Great puffs of steam came from my father's mouth as he huffed and puffed his way through splitting the blocks we'd sawn. Then he'd lean into the woodshed to inspect my stacking.

'Do it right, or you'll do it all again.'

He meant it. There was, in our family, a right way and a

wrong way of doing things. Wood had to be stacked just so. Kindling was chopped only from bone-dry wood.

But I'd get distracted. I loved the smell of the sawdust. When I was young I carried it around by the handful, drawing pictures with it on patches of untouched snow. Woodmen on snowdust. By sprinkling water on it, the picture would eventually be framed in frost. Stacking wood was like doing a vertical jigsaw puzzle. Each piece of wood had its own beauty and I was soon lost in the swirling patterns of knots, or the splotches of lichen on the bark. It was usually dark before I finished.

Arthurs Pass was always my preferred weekend and holiday destination. Much as I liked Akaroa, it was never as satisfying as the alps. It was too easy and there were too many people. At Arthurs Pass the cold had to be dealt with, the mountains needed climbing, the great white slopes cried out to be skied on. The coast was too warm, too pleasant, too small. Nature was too accommodating. Crayfish crawled into the pots at night, flounder swam into the nets, and at low tide the oysters offered themselves on the rocks.

In Akaroa I was accepted because of my family. In the mountains none of that mattered. No family connections could protect you from the icy blasts of sleet, or the ever-present threat of avalanches. The connections I made there were based on skill, not class. I'd go climbing with a plumber from Sydney, a builder's labourer from the West Coast. Where

Akaroa had electricity and sunshine, Arthurs Pass had primus lamps and kerosene burners, oil lamps with wicks that needed trimming. The softer glow of oil lamps has always been more to my liking.

Chapter 5

When I was ten years old I woke one morning and wrote:

> *Distant faces,*
> *lost in black.*
> *Unknown places,*
> *without a track*
> *and the mist at dawn is violent*
> *over a blood-red sea.*
> *Blue grass waves*
> *and blows; intense.*
> *In caverns and caves,*
> *with blood, thick, dense.*
> *Which is green like ink*
> *From a smashed pen*
> *on a broken diary.*

Something was going on inside: the creation of my own mythology.

Between the ages of ten and fifteen I made several attempts to persuade my parents to talk to me about my adoption. Each time I was told not to be so stupid. But being stupid, and stubborn, was something I excelled at.

My school record had been pretty average up until then. I was not a particularly good student and I showed no aptitude for anything other than reading. My ability with numbers did not go much further than basic counting. My writing was illegible even to me. It seems strange that someone who has ended up a writer should have had such problems with English. I left primary school with the worst spelling in my class and no knowledge of grammar other than an understanding that a noun was a 'naming word' and a verb was a 'doing word'. Pronouns? Adverbs? Forget it.

Worse than that, I was losing the capacity I'd had as a young boy to find, by means of intense absorption in some activity, a space deep within myself where I could be at peace. In fact, it was becoming impossible for me to concentrate on anything at all for very long, and with my self-esteem badly battered, I began to crave attention even more. The most obvious impact of this was at school, where my ability to focus was particularly limited and I was easily distracted.

My teachers all implored me to 'try harder', but inside I had frozen up, and at the first hint of failure I became defensive.

I hated not being good at things. I reasoned that if I could only be good at something then people would like me. I so wanted to be liked and loved I would do anything. Except concentrate on my schoolwork.

It was only with hindsight that I understood how traumatised I must have been at the time. The building blocks of my personality had been shattered and I was stumbling through the rubble attempting to make sense of things. School and what I learned there seemed irrelevant. If I couldn't get attention by any other means, I resorted to disruption. It was a strategy that was to prove counter-productive, because while getting into trouble was the surest way of being centre stage, I was also regularly sent from the class, or, at home, to my room.

At Mary McCutcheon's funeral in 1997 a woman came up to me and introduced herself as one of my primary-school teachers.

'What kind of a student was I?' I asked her.

'Difficult,' she replied curtly and walked away.

There was, however, one long-term benefit that came out of this troubled period: I became an avid reader. It was the one thing I could do when sent to my room and one of the few tasks I could concentrate on. The McCutcheon household contained a wonderful library of books, and each time I was banished I would grab a couple to keep me company. At first it was a random selection; one day Rider Haggard, the next Herman Melville. Then I discovered that the books were arranged alphabetically by author, and so began a period of systematic reading; I worked my way from Aesop through to Virginia Woolf.

Although I was as enthralled by Neville Shute as by O Henry, I was lured more by Melpomene than Thalia, and I soon gravitated to the moody Russian and European writers, who for some reason were tucked up together on the top shelves. What a revelation they were: Victor Hugo, Zola, Hesse (particularly his *Magister Ludi*, or *The Glass Bead Game*) and my adolescent favourites, Dostoevsky's *Crime and Punishment* and Turgenev's *Fathers and Sons*. In the latter, the committed radical hero Bazarov was a huge inspiration. His instruction, 'Once you have made a clean sweep, include the ground you're standing on too!' has remained with me ever since.

Slowly but surely my reading began to fuel my search for identity, and following the only lead I had, I turned to non-fiction and consumed everything about World War II that I could get my hands on. I was obsessed with my adoption and the idea that I'd been cheated out of knowing the truth about my heritage. Something in me fastened onto the displaced-persons camps and I became fixated with the notion of dispossession. I was a long way from the truth, but I was not to know that for another forty-odd years.

When as an adolescent I learned about circumcision, I

made an important discovery: only two people I knew had been circumcised. One of them was a boy from a prominent Jewish family and the other one was me. My mind played the cards in order: since I didn't know who I really was but was pretty sure I came from Europe, then it was possible I was Jewish. If the only other circumcised person I knew was Jewish, then there was a fair chance I must be too. If it was true I came from a DP camp . . . It was a line of thinking that sent me off on a tangent which, with hindsight, appears absurd.

I started reading whatever I could about the Jews, and the more I read, the more I felt at home. In retrospect it's clear that this was due to my intense desire to belong to something – anything. With the Jewish emphasis on family, I felt right at ease. Yet when I tried to involve myself with Jewish families in Christchurch, I was given a kind but firm reminder that no matter what I might feel, I was a gentile.

'But I've been circumcised.'

'Many boys are, but not all by a certified Mohel.'

'What's a mole hill?'

'Exactly.'

But after reading *Mein Kampf* and a history of the resistance fighters in the Warsaw Ghetto, it was an easy choice to opt for the Jews over the Nazis. And I became entranced by the literature. The joy of Yiddish humour and of Cabalistic mysticism was seductive, and occupied me when I was supposed to be studying at school. I liked history and geography well enough, but what I really wanted was the history of my marrow, the geography of my village. I wanted my family tree, with my name on a branch. I wanted to discover my ancestors' language. I wanted to know how old I was. And most of all I wanted to know my real name.

I later wrote about this in my play *Night Train*, which ironically won the 1991 Jewish playwrights award – the Samuel Weisberg Award – for which part of the prize was a subscription to *Jewish News*. It still arrives every week. This play was commissioned by the wonderful Jewish actor and director Lenny Kovnor, who on hearing the story of my search for my roots convinced me it was worth writing down. I struggled with the task but was richly rewarded, not only by the Samuel Weisberg prize but by the extraordinary reaction from audiences, even when it was performed as a reading.

I might have had plenty of rebuffs from orthodox Jews, but the more I studied, the more my empathy with Jewish people increased – much to the annoyance of some of my Jewish friends who, while enjoying my company, thought I was a little touched. Yet over the years – first in New Zealand and Europe and later, for a short time, in the smallest and oldest synagogue in Australia – I got to know some wonderful people who didn't give a damn whether I had been circumcised by a rabbinic Mohel or by the local butcher.

Things didn't get any better at high school, where I had days of torture to endure: Latin with Mr Bennet, French with Mr Dowling, and maths with a master whose name I have thankfully erased.

I enjoyed my first encounter with Latin, a language that held the key to unlocking English words, and I was having a love affair with words. Yet my troubled primary-school years had left me ill-equipped to parse a sentence, even in English, and I stumbled over nominative, genitive and dative cases. By the time I reached ablative, locative and vocative, I was flat on my face.

I had similar problems with French, which were compounded by a personality clash between Mr Dowling and myself. His nickname was Dryballs, and his nasal twang was irritating, his imperious lecturing infuriating. In a moment of madness that elicited gasps from my classmates, I asked him if he would please talk *with* us, rather than lecture *at* us. It was the beginning of a war in which my application to the French language was the first casualty.

'You defy me, boy, and I'll defy you!' he once roared, whirling on me, his gown and nostrils flaring.

'I was just asking —' I began. But his hand was up, pointing towards his study.

'Go now!'

The wait seemed interminable, but eventually he came in and selected a cane from beside his desk. He had a charming manner of applying it to my rear.

'Bend over and watch the flowers on the floor, boy.'

I gritted my teeth and stared at the floral carpet. Dryballs might have been a brilliant French scholar but his maths was no better than mine. He appeared to know only one number: six. Six of the best, he called it. Best for what? Humiliation? Pain? I loathed him and French more with every stroke. I have hated floral carpet ever since.

Mathematics was to me another foreign language, one I had no desire to learn. At the time, I could conceive of no circumstance in my adult life where I would need it, and my abysmal results reflected a highly developed and genuine lack of interest. Unfortunately my failure at numeracy flowed over to two other subjects I did enjoy, chemistry and physics. The deeper we delved into the physical sciences, the more important maths became, and the lower my marks dipped. Mac McCutcheon was less than impressed.

There were bright spots. I was fortunate in having a very talented history teacher who encouraged my interest in the subject, one that has remained with me all my life. He taught me not just to learn the dates but to look at the patterns and the big picture. And with the convictions I held about my background, I had a very personal investment in studying history.

Despite my lack of basic grammar and spelling, English came naturally to me, and though I couldn't have cared if an infinitive was split or splattered, I still managed very good marks. What I lost on the grammar questions I more than made up for in comprehension and essay writing, winning the school essay prize in 1964.

Outside the classroom, I was a member of the debating team, where I shone, and the choir. Though I remained untouched by the religious content of the choir's repertoire, I was moved by the alchemy that took place when the harmonies soared around the school's beautiful chapel.

The dark side of school was the bike shed. It was there that most of the bullying took place. A couple of boys had discovered that the best way to release stress at the end of a day of frustrations and reprimands was to beat up someone smaller. As I was small for my age, I was an obvious victim. I was an annoying enough kid to become a target, and I was also a smart-arse who did stupid things like excel in public speaking and debating.

Being in the choir was also a matter of concern for my persecutors, raising questions about my masculinity. And then there was the poetry thing. I'd made the fatal mistake of not only writing it but showing off my expertise when asked to recite in class. It only took one teacher to compliment me and I was fair game for kids who thought it was sissy to muck around with words.

It seemed to me that bullying was institutionalised at St Andrew's in those days. The teachers bullied the students, the prefects bullied the students, and the students bullied those younger or smarter than they were. I was right at the bottom of the pecking order and not blessed with the desire to bully anyone. Ironically, the one thing I could rely on as a defence was my knack with words, and I sometimes managed to talk my way out of trouble.

Afternoons were hell. As the clock crept through treacle towards the final bell, I would prepare myself for the dash to the bike shed. If I made it before the bullies I would cycle off with great relief. If I didn't I would get punched, kicked and jeered at.

One boy in particular took great exception to my 'showing off'. Alan was bigger, faster and stronger than me by a long way. What he lacked academically he made up for in sporting prowess. There was another boy, Geoff, who considered himself a friend of mine, who would wait patiently for the beating to stop, and then – and this is something that continues to astonish me – we would all ride home together, Alan, Geoff and me. The three musketeers.

The bike ride would be fine. We would talk about other things, and Alan, away from his cohorts, would be as nice as pie. He later volunteered for service in Vietnam. I haven't heard anything of him since.

It didn't help that I was mediocre at school sports. I was a fast but wildly inaccurate cricket bowler, much better at hockey, and atrocious at rugby. The other boys used me for kicking practice. If skiing had been a school sport back then,

I might have been a sporting hero. Skiing was my passion, and the only endeavour in which I felt completely at home. It was something I'd done since the age of four and there wasn't an aspect of it I didn't enjoy. No matter whether I was racing, skiing with others or alone, I was in heaven.

My lifelong friend Guy Hargreaves remembers hearing rumours of my skiing before he met me at the age of thirteen. We were both competing in the Canterbury Junior Championship at Amuri, north of Christchurch, and Guy, despite having a home-field advantage, was concerned that his crown would be stolen. It didn't happen. Guy won by several seconds and we became firm friends.

Guy lived just around the corner from our house in Fendalton and he remained a solid and dependable friend throughout my troubled teenage years. His mother kept an open house for me, a refuge when I needed to escape, and I spent a lot of time there. The older I got, the more claustrophobic school and home life became. To protect myself from my father's increasing anger at my social and academic failures, I attempted to enlist the company of others on our weekends away, but most of my friends were intimidated by Mac. One described him as 'overbearing and chilling'. Guy was less generous, recalling him years later as 'vindictive'.

To his credit, Guy, knowing how much it helped me, tried on a couple of occasions to spend a weekend with my family, both at Arthurs Pass and Akaroa. But the more time he spent near Mac, the more he feared and disliked him, and after witnessing shouting scenes and the hurling of a marble ashtray at my head, he opted to stay out of the way.

Guy also tells the story of a knife being thrown, but I have no memory of that, and he makes the interesting observation, echoed by others, that my mother was much softer when Mac wasn't around, leading Guy to believe that she too was frightened of his rages. While there may be some truth in the notion that Mary found Mac's anger difficult to deal with, I find it hard to believe she was frightened of anything. There was, beneath her mild exterior, a rapier-sharp mind, and a strength of will to accompany it.

Guy and I shared a strong link apart from skiing. He too had lost his father, who'd been a British spy during World War II. After parachuting behind enemy lines in Yugoslavia, he was captured and sent to the infamous Colditz Castle prisoner-of-war camp, where he remained until the end of the war. On his release he went to New Zealand, married and had two children. But he was deeply traumatised by his wartime experiences, particularly his treatment in captivity, and shortly afterwards he abandoned his family and returned to England. Guy did not see his father again until he was in his twenties.

This wasn't something we ever discussed when we were young, but it helped form an unspoken bond between us. And we also had another connection, one that no amount of parental interference could break: Guy once saved my life.

When we were in our teens he and I would go skiing on weekends at Arthurs Pass without my family. One Friday we headed out of Christchurch on the evening train, arriving late at night. The walk from the station to the ski-club hut where we were staying was several kilometres, and it was well after midnight when we started the final ascent. Both of us were carrying heavy packs, skis and ski boots. After about an hour of climbing, we were suddenly hit by a snowstorm.

Subzero winds and white-out conditions are dangerous at any time, but when you're exhausted they can be fatal. The approach to the hut was a long, exposed ridge with treacherous ravines on either side. Normally the path was discernible in the dark, but we now found ourselves floundering in deep snow, with little idea of our bearings. I began to feel drowsy. All I wanted to do was lie down and rest.

The early-warning signs of hypothermia had been drilled into both of us from a young age, and yet they're so insidious that once they manifest themselves you're beyond reason. Left to my own devices I would have simply given up and frozen to death, but Guy was not as exhausted as I was and instantly recognised what was happening. He swore and yelled at me, dragging me forward, and then, exasperated by my immobility, he wrenched my skis from me and added them to his own load. Cursing and shoving me, he pushed on through the blizzard.

We managed to remain on the ridge, and half an hour later found ourselves outside the hut. Once inside, Guy lit a fire and made hot drinks that soon revived me. It was a close call, and could so easily have ended in tragedy had Guy not been so perceptive, and so stubborn.

When I was around eighteen or nineteen the dreams started. I had three that recurred for a period of more than twenty years, until the mid-1980s. They were quite distinct: flying dreams, dreams of wolves, and an epic, ever-expanding dream of trains in European landscapes. The train dreams – inspired, I am certain, by my having read so much about refugees in Europe – became not only the fuel for short stories and plays, but also a metaphor for my search.

In the dream I am a young boy again. It is night and I am hurtling on a train through a foreign landscape. It is a landscape I am aware of but can not see. Outside there are few lights and much darkness. Glinting rain whips across the smoke-stained window. Everything has been swallowed up by the night. All that is certain has been left behind in some forgotten siding, and now, with no luggage and no destination, I simply travel. I live on the train. I move in order to stay in front of myself. I am searching for a ghost. My travelling companions are the nomads and the gypsies, the misfits, the pimps and poets, the beautiful losers.

A rabbi asks me, 'Why is this night different from any other night?'

'Tonight we came out of the land of Egypt.'

'No,' says a woman in a black headscarf. 'No, they never made it out of Warsaw. I saw them in the Old City, not far from Krashinsky Square. She was cooking a potato between the hot bricks of a burnt-out building. Her fingers were black, chafed from sorting through the rubble, looking for her children.'

The woman starts to walk away, then glances at me and shakes her head. 'Wake up to yourself, boy. Remember who you are.'

The train stops deep in a forest and I fade through the side of the carriage and land in thick snow. On either side of the train are shadows fragmented by moonlight – moonlight strained through swaying spruce and alder. The cold is so intense it freezes breath to face and yet it is exhilarating. I pause in a space between the dark and the cold and understanding, and I realise that the answers lie on the train, not off it – outside the train is distraction and more forgetting. I look up and see behind pale frosted glass the haunted faces of mothers searching the blackness for their children . . .

Variations on this dream haunted me for years. Then, for no reason that I can fathom, they stopped. All the wanting – the longing for a tribe, a hearth, a home – was suddenly no more than a search for a grave marked, in whatever language, 'Mother'.

Chapter 6

When I hit puberty my internal confusion found itself competing with a more elemental rival: testosterone. Those times when my hormones were in the ascendancy, my deep-seated sadness and feelings of abandonment seemed to take a back seat. But perhaps the most marked effect of being abandoned is an overarching desire to be loved, and with hindsight I think I simply shifted the focus of that desire. New territory was opening up, and I was no longer restricted to my family for the fulfilment of my desperate yearning to be the centre of attention.

Of course this was a recipe for disaster. Transferring such entrenched needs from a family to a girlfriend was, I soon found, far from ideal as a basis for a relationship. Initially the girls I was attracted to seemed to find my hormone-enhanced attentions flattering, but the moment they were exposed to my underlying neediness they very sensibly dumped me. Even though this pattern was repeated again and again, I was slow to learn from it and continued to throw myself into very one-sided romances.

Adding to the heartbreak of these affairs was the depth of my reaction to each rejection. Every time a relationship ended I was plunged into a self-centred melancholy, fuelled by my ingrained sense of abandonment. Making matters worse was the habit I developed of attaching myself not only to a girlfriend but also her family, particularly her mother. So whenever a romance ended I lost another family.

In the early 1960s a muse intervened and changed things. The muse came in the form of a school teacher (not from my own school) who, during an agonisingly short week at a ski-club hut, she gave me a one-on-one sex education. I received intense instruction in what – according to the teacher, anyway – pleased a woman. How to make love with or for, but never to, a woman. She was ten years older than I was and vastly more experienced; it was mind-boggling. Of course I still had a deep craving to be loved, but the revelation that the best way to get love and attention was to give it made a profound impression.

Years later, when I confided this to a friend, they were shocked, saying it was tantamount to sexual abuse. I disagreed then and I still do now. To me it was a blessing. The initiation of young boys into the art of sex by experienced older women has a lot to recommend it.

It's easy to dismiss teenage sexuality as experimentation that doesn't ultimately mean anything, but for me each experience, no matter how transitory or innocent, was important – yet another expression of my yearning to be loved and to belong. Each encounter had the potential to fill the void left by the missing piece of the jigsaw puzzle. When relationships ended, the pain revived my awareness of abandonment. There was never a relationship whose demise I didn't grieve over.

Much of my childhood may be hazy in my mind, but those adolescent moments of intimate connection remain crystal clear. A circle of us youngsters, our faces glowing in the light of an oil lamp or a candle, crouching on the floor at Arthurs Pass, playing spin the bottle. The girl who got tangled with me in my bicycle, falling to the ground during one of my clumsy attempts to kiss her after church one Sunday.

The first girl I was seriously smitten by was as nervous as I was. In the snow at Arthurs Pass, she huffed on my glasses so that I couldn't look at her while she kissed me. Libby Hamilton was the first great love of my life, and we fitted the social script. She was the daughter of a Canterbury farmer, I the son of a Christchurch professional. What wasn't in the script was that we were both so young. We had known each other from a very early age but we would have been thirteen or fourteen when our romance began.

Naturally things had to be kept secret, so we arranged clandestine meetings in a forest clearing behind her parents' house. This was at the opposite end of the pass to our cottage, and I had to not only give my parents a good excuse for going out, but trek through the snow for a brief fifteen minutes of extremely innocent hugging and kissing – pashing, as it was known back then.

Longer dates were harder to organise because Libby's father patrolled her virtue like a prison warder. But a friend of hers came to our rescue. She would collect Libby from her house and bring her to our hiding place in the forest, then move some ten yards away and wait, back turned, until we were finished.

Back in Christchurch, Libby went to Cashmere High School and boarded with a family who, inconsiderately, lived at the top of a valley at Hoon Hay. This tested my love to the extreme; Fendalton was in the north of the city and Hoon Hay was about as south as you could go without climbing the Cashmere Hills. Libby and I spent hours talking on the phone, but I was so smitten that I would regularly get on my bicycle and ride the twelve or so kilometres out to Hoon Hay for a few stolen moments at the front gate. Libby was worth every aching kilometre.

On one occasion I did manage to arrange a serious date, and I persuaded my parents to drive out to Hoon Hay and pick up Libby so we could go to the pictures together. It was the strangest evening, because my parents insisted on accompanying us.

Libby and I never did anything but kiss. Some of my schoolmates were already boasting about their sexual conquests, whereas I didn't get much further than a hand up her blouse. I don't think I even tried. Through all this, though, there was never an invitation to the heart of what I craved most – Libby's family. As much as I liked the daughter, I yearned for the affection of her mother.

Self-destructive by nature, and with my nose for trouble already well developed, I owe it more to luck than skill that I avoided any serious trouble as a teenager. The closest I came to it arose from my discovery of the more rebellious side of Christchurch nightlife.

By the early 1960s the youthful rebellion against straight-laced Christchurch society was beginning to gnaw at the very centre of the city. A group of actors took over the seedy King Bee Koffee Keller, adjacent to Cathedral Square, and renamed it the Stage Door Club. This dank venue in Hereford Lane epitomised everything my parents' generation hated and feared: a couple of hundred young people high on drink, drugs and music. During the week there was poetry and folk music; on weekends the music was anarchic and wild. A local band, The Chants, had us all bouncing off the rafters. Hipflasks of booze were passed around, as were pills, joints, and medical morphine stolen from fishing boats in Lyttelton. In those days, morphine and other narcotics were still carried in first-aid kits by commercial fishermen.

In such an atmosphere the social barriers came down. Musicians, long-haired bikers and actors mixed with dissolute kids and private-school girls out to get stoned and laid. For a kid from Fendalton, the Stage Door Club was a revelation. It was another world, the world I had been warned about.

Also in the heart of the city, in Cashel Street, was the 77 Club, a bohemian dive. From the moment I found it I was hooked. With its jazz, its seedy patrons, illicit alcohol and drugs, it too stood for everything my parents despised. Not only were many of its pleasures illegal, but the heated debates and conversations that took place there were about subjects that Mac and Mary would have considered absolute rubbish at best, dangerously subversive at worst. For me it was the perfect rebellion against an authoritarian family, school, and even the city itself. But sustaining my rebellion proved to be a risky undertaking.

My parents, of course, would not have sanctioned my going to such a place under any circumstances. I had another problem in that nothing really happened at the club until very late at night or the early hours of the morning, and I also had very little money to pay for anything other than getting in the door.

Nevertheless I was determined, and having oiled every moving part on my bike, along with the hinges on my bedroom window, I would dress in the obligatory beatnik black and make my escape. Sneaking out the window and riding into the city at such an hour was perilous, considering how Mac would have reacted had he discovered what I was up to, but this added to the potency of the experience. The frisson of danger kept me on edge from the moment I left home until I returned.

At the club I would sit with one eye on the stairs, half expecting Mac to come storming up them at any moment. There'd be an explosive scene and I'd be dragged away and thrashed. But somehow I was never caught. Limiting myself to a couple of mid-week excursions, I would arrive home in time to get a few hours' sleep before school, and there was the added bonus of the approval I got from Mary for my devotion to getting to bed early.

The smoky atmosphere of the 77 Club, the late-night jazz and the weird and wonderful patrons were the antithesis of everything I had known to date. I met people who discussed Sartre, Proust and Kafka. They drank whisky neat out of battered hipflasks, smoked reefers (how quaint that term seems now) and talked politics. They raved and ranted. They swore. This was rebellion writ large. To sit around with adults who were seriously interested in whether 'existence precedes essence', or the fact that 'subjectivity must be the turning point' was as exciting as it was inexplicable. Did these people have jobs? What did *their* parents think?

In the background a blind multi-instrumentalist would play beautiful music. Claude Papesch, originally from New Plymouth, had been one of the Devils in New Zealand's first rock'n'roll band, Johnny Devlin and the Devils. When I met him in the early 1960s he had toured far and wide and it was a mystery to me why he should be playing in the 77 Club. It wasn't long before I learned just how hard it was to make a living in the arts, but back then I was still naïve.

I was scared of Claude. Probably because I didn't know how to relate to a blind person, but also because of the unpredictable nature of the man. I got enough of that at home. One memorable night he tipped a jukebox down the stairs onto a Maori bouncer with whom he was brawling. For a blind man his aim was pretty good. Mind you, it'd be hard to miss with an object the size of a jukebox. Yet when he played the keyboard, or put his lips to the saxophone, he could paint pictures in the air.

Another night, emboldened by a shot of Scotch in my coffee, I boasted to Claude that I could extemporise poetry. For a moment Claude did a bloody good impression of looking at me.

'Yeah? Cool.' He turned back to his keyboard and handed me a microphone. 'Give us some, kid.'

I was scared shitless, but as Claude began to play, the words tumbled out. The drummer, Bruno Lawrence, drifted back to his kit and eased a brush over the snare, and for about ten minutes I experienced what it was like to be a part of the music. It flowed around me in a way that was so exhilarating that for a while there was nothing else. Then, as suddenly as it had started, it was over. To my amazement there was scattered applause. I turned red and fled to the toilets.

From then on I got to perform a couple of times a week, for which I earned an amazing amount of money, five pounds a night. On top of that I was no longer paying for coffee. I was intoxicated by my success.

I eventually lost touch with Claude, but I struck up a friendship with Bruno. Years later he and I reconnected in Australia and we'd meet up from time to time. He had gone on to have a remarkable career as an actor and musician and is probably best remembered by Australians for his role in the television series *Frontline*. But his performances in films like *Smash Palace*, *Grievous Bodily Harm*, *The Quiet Earth* and *Utu* are just as memorable.

It was only after Bruno's death in 1995 that I discovered what happened to Claude. He had settled in New South Wales, where he'd continued playing jazz and served on the Lithgow City Council. He was elected mayor in 1984 but died of cancer in 1987. He was forty-five.

Around 1963 the 77 Club closed and my clubbing days were over, but one man I met there was to have a profound and ongoing effect on me. Jack forced me to think about every aspect of life in political terms. To a young and impressionable Christchurch lad, he was exotic. He was not only American, he was a devout communist.

Jack was a wisp of a man. Tall and stiff but insubstantial. Balding, with a neat grey goatee. His normal manner of address was to spit out short sentences like rapid bursts from a machine gun. He introduced himself to me with: '"I saw the best minds of my generation destroyed by madness, starving hysterical naked . . ."'

I didn't know what to say.

'Ginsberg,' he spluttered. 'Brilliant.' He handed me a small book and said, 'You'll enjoy it. You'll enjoy Sandra. Address is in the front. Just drop in any time. I want to introduce you to Trotsky.'

It occurred to me that maybe he hadn't heard Trotsky was dead, but before I could say anything he patted me on the arm and departed. I tucked the book into my coat pocket and forgot about it for several days.

When I finally got around to reading it I discovered it was a badly printed version of Allen Ginsberg's seminal poem *Howl*, written in the mid-1950s. I read it during lunch break at school and hardly understood a word of it. Yet I came back to it time and again in the next couple of weeks and found myself intoxicated and affronted at the same time. This was not poetry as I knew or comprehended it, but I felt it was a doorway to somewhere I needed to visit.

On a Saturday morning a few weeks later, I picked up the book, checked the address and decided to visit. Jack lived in the beachside suburb of Sumner, and after catching a bus into the city then out again on the Sumner route, I set about hunting down his house.

In those days the homes in Sumner couldn't have been more different from Fendalton's. This was not the locale for stately houses and manicured gardens, and I eventually found myself standing outside a weatherboard dwelling in desperate need of attention. The garden, if you could call it such, was little more than a collection of weeds. What passed for a lawn had not been cut in a long time.

The front door was ajar, and when I knocked it was opened by a woman as large and loud as her American accent. She was in her forties, with long grey hair swept over her shoulder and covering one side of her face. I thought myself a worldly seventeen-year-old, but I was transfixed by the sight of her large breasts floating freely under a loose blouse.

'You're the poet?' the woman asked when I gave my name. She seemed oblivious to my discomfort.

A poet? Yes, that felt good. I must have nodded, because the next moment I was kissed on the cheek and swept inside.

'I'm Naomi,' she said, and squeezed past me to lead the way between a pile of boxes. 'Jack will be back shortly, so come in. Careful you don't trip over our junk.'

Nothing in my experience prepared me for their house.

Every available space was taken up by things. Cupboards overflowed; papers and books spilled from shelves and were piled against the walls; boxes and trunks, open and closed, were jammed in between coffee tables constructed from bricks and planks. On the window ledges, pot plants were either dead from neglect or cascaded down to join the rest of the muddle. The place was a chaotic mix of fecundity and decay in equal doses; it seemed impossible that it could be home to a functioning family. Surely this chaos was a sign of deeper trouble?

Naomi swept some folders off a chair and plonked herself down. 'Shall I tell you all about us?' she asked, and without waiting for a reply she launched into a diatribe against the evil and oppressive empire that was the United States of Amerika. 'I spell it with a "k",' she explained.

I was mesmerised, not only by her enthusiasm for the topic, but by the increasingly frequent glimpses of her breasts, which were intent on escaping the oppression of her blouse. The family had fled America because of a deeply held conviction that the world was about to suffer a nuclear disaster. Their house in Sumner was only a temporary camp; they'd purchased land on the rugged West Coast and were building a place in which to survive the forthcoming cataclysm. My mind flashed back to Neville Shute. His *On the Beach* had a lot to answer for.

Jack and Naomi were a wonderful double act, with the

ability to finish each other's sentences, at times in unison, but their daughter Sandra couldn't have been more different. A couple of years older than me, she was almost as tall as her father, but whereas he was slightly stiff she was as lithe as a ballet dancer. She was mercury to his steel. In her few short years Sandra had managed to achieve an advanced state of ennui that she wore like a crown. Silent, dark-haired and with remarkable green eyes, she draped herself across chairs rather than in them, and though she rarely contributed she always remained present while her mother and father launched themselves into their Trotskyist dissertations. From time to time Sandra would catch my gaze and roll her eyes in mock anguish.

No matter how desperately I wanted to connect with Jack and Naomi, somehow I couldn't get enthused about the writings and notions of a man who'd died with an icepick in his brain. I had explored the worlds of Hitler and Stalin and found them equally repugnant, and years later I would have fierce disagreements with people who tried to paint Trotsky as the softer alternative to Stalin. They were both murderers, in my opinion.

I fought with Jack about Stalin's pact with Hitler, but I was punching way out of my league. Jack was a polished orator and debater; you did not win arguments with him, you merely ignited a new set of debates. Yet when we strayed into the minefield of moral equivalence, I held my own, arguing that the millions killed in the Soviet Union *were* different from the Shoah. But I was ill equipped, and although I had a feeling for my argument, I didn't have at my command anything approaching the stunning phrase that years later Martin Amis coined to describe his emotional response to the holocaust: 'species shame'.

In the early 1980s, when I thought Trotskyists were well and truly extinct, I was to run into one again. I was in London for a rehearsal of my play *The Truce*. Because it was set in Warsaw immediately after the Polish Uprising, the director and I decided that the cast would benefit from watching Andrzej Wajda's film *Ashes and Diamonds*. We hired a theatre in Soho and held a private screening. Afterwards one of the actresses, who had arrived in a chauffeur-driven Bentley, asked me if I would like to go and have a cup of tea while she waited for her driver.

While we were sipping our cuppa, she produced a copy of the *Socialist Worker* and offered to sell it to me. I was so astounded I agreed. Then, as her car hove into view, I discovered that my companion was short of cash to pay for the tea. Not a problem, I assured her. Clutching my *Socialist Worker* under one arm, I waved goodbye to her as she climbed into the Bentley: the last of the old Trots, Vanessa Redgrave.

While communism was the bond that kept the juices flowing for Jack and Naomi, poetry was the only thing that raised Sandra out of her torpor. Over those few short weeks she introduced me to Lawrence Ferlinghetti, Gregory Corso and William Carlos Williams, and I loved her for it. When, at her parents' urging, I arranged to stay over on a Saturday night, I discovered that Sandra was not as complex as I had imagined her to be. Picking up on Naomi's winks and nudges, she shunted me towards her bedroom and proclaimed me to be a 'little bourgeois twerp'. While the sex was great, she later broke down and cried. What she really wanted, she said between sniffles, was to go home to her friends in California.

I lost contact with Jack and his family when they moved to the West Coast, but they left me a valuable legacy. Although I'd already begun flirting with ideas beyond those found in the claustrophobic community of Fendalton, it was Jack and Naomi who opened the door to more radical concepts. Rebellion, they showed me, could be much more substantial than a fuel for late-night discussions. It could be a way of life.

Chapter 7

On leaving school my strongest desire was to get out of New Zealand as fast as possible. At seventeen I was still obsessed with the search for my roots but now my quest was entering a new phase. Suddenly I was a free agent; I could go to Europe, where I believed there was a chance of finding my real mother. Or where, if I was unable to find her, I might at least hear and instinctively recognise my mother tongue.

My reading about displaced-persons camps, death camps and slave-labour camps had not abated. I devoured everything I could, amassing facts and figures that I somehow thought would come together like pieces of the jigsaw: the number of prisoners at Majdanek, the nationalities of the inmates of Ravensbrück, the date of liberation of the children's camp at Uckermark ... Facts, cold hard facts, but of course behind each of them was a story. A tragedy. The pain of what I learned engulfed me, and at times I had horrific nightmares about those places.

Information on the concentration camps was not difficult to come by. The displaced-persons camps were a different story – simply finding their names and locations was a huge task. In 1948 in Germany alone there were just under four hundred DP camps, and there were another 120 in Austria. During my research I came across a brochure called 'DPs are People', which had been distributed by a church group. It read in part:

> There are 850,000 still in camps who can never go home ... Poles, Latvians, Lithuanians, Estonians, Yugoslavs, Greeks, Ukrainians, Czechoslovaks. Brought into Germany as slave labourers and concentration camp inmates, they can not return to their Soviet-dominated lands because of fear of political and religious persecution ... Over 150,000 children, at least half of them under the age of six, live in these camps. Fifty per cent of all DPs are women and children.

That was written in 1948. If indeed I was one of those displaced children, I would have been around eighteen months old at the time. The international refugee organisations had done great work assisting people to find homes around the globe, but, like the Red Cross, they could give no information on those they'd helped unless you had at least a surname. Several times I asked Mary McCutcheon to tell me what my real name was, but each time I was rebuffed, and exhorted to 'stop all this silliness'. Perhaps I should have listened, because the task was impossible.

So the first thing I did after leaving school was to start saving for a trip to London. Confident that once there I would find work as an actor, I planned to buy only a one-way ticket. My desire for a life in theatre had not abated. At primary school I had written and starred in my own one-boy show, of which there was a single performance, and at high school I became seriously engaged by the power of theatre to explore ideas. In my upper-sixth year I was cast in Luigi Pirandello's *Six Characters in Search of an Author*.

In this play a theatrical company in rehearsal are interrupted by a man and his family who explain that they are characters from an unfinished dramatic work. The son refuses to acknowledge his family and runs into the garden, where he shoots himself. The remaining actors argue about whether the boy is dead or not. The father insists the events are real. The producer says, 'Make-believe? Reality? Oh, go to hell the lot of you! Lights! Lights! Lights!'

It was little wonder the play resonated with me. After a public performance our family doctor made a point of telling me and Mac McCutcheon that I had a talent worth fostering.

While Mac would have none of it, I was deeply affected by this praise, coming as it did at a time when my relationship with my parents was particularly bad. As far as they were concerned, my school marks were abysmal and I was headed for a second-rate life. They told me so in no uncertain terms.

I seemed to have no aptitude for anything except writing and performing. Several actors from the Christchurch Repertory Theatre who had seen my school performances encouraged me to consider theatre as a professional option, but I might never have been convinced to follow a career on the stage had it not been for an invitation to audition for an open-air production of the York Cycle of Mystery Plays with the British actor Jonathan Eltham.

My audition was successful, and as far as I'm aware, that production was the first time the cycle was performed in New Zealand. This, combined with the location chosen for the staging, ensured that it was well attended. The set was built against the backdrop of the picturesque stone buildings of the Christchurch law courts on the banks of the River Avon. On the opposite side of the river, seating that looked liked rugby stands was constructed for the audience.

The parts I played were minuscule – Roman Soldier number eighteen, for example – but it was an exhilarating experience nevertheless. One night I came onstage to find the audience a sea of black and white. The show had been booked out entirely by nuns.

Being swept up in the company of real actors in a successful production was a great feeling, and when Jonathon Eltham was kind enough to say that he thought I should pursue a stage career I was hooked. For me the allure of theatre was multi-faceted. Naturally I loved being in the spotlight, but more than anything I relished the fact that on stage I could be someone other than who I was. For a brief time each night I was transported out of myself, and the only identity that mattered was the one I created under lights.

At that time there was no professional theatre in New Zealand and it was hard to find paid work as an actor other than in radio dramas. The only option for someone wanting a career on the stage was to go overseas, a path taken by many of New Zealand's best actors. I decided to follow, but a short stint as a copywriter after leaving school made it obvious that I needed a better income if I was to depart New Zealand any time soon.

Moreover, while the people I worked with in the Ingles-Wright Advertising Agency were convinced they were at the cutting edge of creativity, I found writing copy for radio and press advertisements soul-destroying. So I quit the job and headed to the country town of Cheviot, where for a year I worked as part of a nassella-tussock gang.

Nassella tussock is a weed, a single plant of which can produce up to 120 000 seeds a year, which are dispersed over long distances by wind, water, animals and humans. Hour after hour, day after day, we scoured hillsides, grubbing out weeds with mattocks. It was hot, dirty work. My companions were a mixed bunch of dropouts and recently released criminals.

After a drinking bout, the camp chef was fired and I was elected cook. This was a great relief from the backbreaking work in the sun but had one minor drawback. I didn't know how to cook. Then I remembered those large pots of porridge at the ski schools at Arthurs Pass and decided it couldn't be all that hard. With a great deal of bluff and good luck I soon had it nailed.

Mac and Mary McCutcheon saw my decision to do such manual labour as further proof that I had gone completely off the rails. They had taken my refusal to go to university as a slap in the face, a rejection of the good schooling they'd paid for. To them my behaviour was insulting, and a betrayal. By the time I went to work in Cheviot they had no doubt despaired of me ever coming to my senses. They grimly predicted that my life would be a disaster. But by then I no longer cared what they thought.

At first life in Cheviot was very quiet. I rose before dawn each day to prepare breakfast for the men and then, apart from shopping for supplies, I had nothing to do before preparing the evening meal. I soon became proficient at producing huge quantities of porridge, roast meat, baked vegetables and gravy. Eventually even my custards were lump-free.

Things changed when I met Gabrielle, a bright eighteen-year-old who'd grown tired of being cooped up in a country town and who saw me as her chance to leave. Our relationship ignited like a summer grass fire, with only one dampening aspect. As a well-brought-up Catholic she was firmly committed to remaining a virgin until she was married.

We nevertheless spent an idyllic summer and planned to travel before eventually settling down together. I had already booked and paid a deposit on a ticket to England, and as Gabrielle was unable to get a berth on the same ship, we made plans to meet in Southampton. There was little to spend money on in Cheviot, and after purchasing an engagement ring for Gabrielle I soon had enough to pay off my passage on the Shaw Savill liner, *Northern Star*.

It was at this time that I first saw a copy of my birth certificate, which I needed in order to apply for a passport. When the certificate arrived from the Office of the Registrar of Births, Deaths and Marriages I was taken aback by its brevity. The name on it was the one I'd formally grown up with – Robert Hamish McCutcheon – but apart from a date of birth, which was also the one I'd grown up with, it gave no details. There was no mention of any parents.

I took solace in the thought that somewhere in Europe was my motherland, my mother tongue, and maybe even my mother. The convention at the time among *pakeha* (non-Maori) New Zealanders to refer to a trip to Europe as 'going home' felt particularly apposite to me.

Gabrielle went with me to Auckland, from where my ship set sail, and there was an intensely emotional moment as she stood on the wharf waving goodbye, to the accompaniment of The Seekers' 'The Carnival is Over' on the loudspeakers.

Once the ship was in open waters I felt like I'd been set free. It was as though I were leaving not just New Zealand but also the person I'd been up to that point – not an uncommon experience for anyone going overseas for the first time. I was young, it was the sixties, and I had escaped. The journey, via Rarotonga, Tahiti, Acapulco, Panama City, Trinidad, Lisbon and Southampton, became a rite of passage in every sense of the term. I gave little thought to anything but the moment – certainly not to my engagement – and between Tahiti and Panama I indulged in everything my McCutcheon upbringing had taught me to resist. It was wonderful.

When we got to Tahiti I was guided by over-friendly locals to a dive called Quinn's Bar, where the combination of the exotic atmosphere and rum conspired to deliver me into the experienced hands of a woman whose occupation and intentions were not immediately clear to a naïve New Zealander. I clearly remember her name: Maria. After a couple of drinks Maria confided that it would be far less expensive to continue the evening at her place. This turned out to be little more than a shack, but I spent an enjoyably indulgent night which included, among other things, great conversation and a game of chess, which we concluded as the sun came up. Touchingly,

Maria came down to the harbour to see me off. From what I hear from others, service like that is now a thing of the past.

Acapulco was less inspiring, although I was struck by the readiness of almost every young boy there to offer me his sister in return for a biro or a fountain pen. I'm sure there must have been more to it than that but I didn't have enough stationery supplies to find out. The high point of the voyage was Panama City. Here the locals were world leaders at fleecing tourists, but I was fortunate to have hooked up on the ship with an experienced traveller who had a set of survival tactics for any situation.

'When we dock,' he informed me, 'there'll be dozens of people offering their services as guides. Pick one, and when he tells you how much he charges, offer him double. Pay half in advance, then insist he accompany you for the entire night.'

It was good advice. The guide I selected introduced himself as 'my old friend Sylvester and I can show you Panama exhibition', and when I put it to him that he could earn more by sticking with me all evening, he grinned and said, 'Ah, you have been here before.'

Sylvester's transport turned out to be a retired US army jeep with no roof or side panels. As we clambered in he pulled out a joint, lit it and handed it to me, yelling over the noise of the engine that we were going to have a 'very excellently beautiful time in old Panama'.

We drove at high speed out of the American zone, through

back roads to an isolated and dilapidated colonial mansion, where off-duty American servicemen made quick cash by supplying almost every vice known to man. This was the home of the infamous 'exhibition'. I might have been naïve but even I knew that it would be something less salubrious than an art show. Nevertheless I was still genuinely shocked to be shown a room with several hundred Americans being entertained by a group of tired whores attempting to coax a bored donkey into various sex acts.

The rest of the night was a blur of high-quality dope, low-priced brothels, dancing, great music and Sylvester's laughter, which was, it later transpired to my great relief, the only infectious thing about the evening. True to his word he delivered me back to the ship exhausted but happy as dawn broke. As a parting gift he pressed a large lump of hashish into my hand.

By the time my eighteenth birthday came around, we were approaching Lisbon, where on an impulse I took my backpack and sleeping-bag and disembarked. This was Europe and I felt that I had come home. The *Northern Star* and my luggage sailed on to Southampton and I never saw either of them again. Such an impetuous and irrational act I can only put down to a Kerouac-inspired desire to be on the road. I made no attempt to retrieve my luggage – it contained clothes that belonged to my former Christchurch life, and they no longer seemed appropriate.

Portugal was all heat and sunshine and I set off hitch-hiking down the coast, living on fruit from citrus orchards and camping on beaches, doing it rough. I had no understanding of Portuguese, no local knowledge whatsoever, but life as Dean Moriarty was fine – until I contracted a severe case of sunstroke. At some point I collapsed, and my next memory is of a kindly gentleman driving me back to Lisbon and depositing me at a hospital.

Fortunately I recovered quickly, after which I set out for Spain. Just over the border my luck ran out and I spent two whole days trying to thumb a lift. Eventually an eccentric character named Henry picked me up in his Mini Minor and took me most of the way to Madrid. Having an English father and Spanish mother, Henry's English was impeccable and he invited me to stay at his parents' house in Madrid, but he couldn't take me all the way because he had to make a detour to his brother's place in the countryside. As he dropped me off the rain started, and I counted myself lucky to get a lift with a truck driver who was going straight through to Madrid.

It turned out to be not so lucky. At the time, General Franco was offering a bonus to drivers who delivered fish from the coast to the capital in quick time: fine for the driver, maybe, but I have never been as terrified as I was on that high-speed run into Madrid. I made it to the city but not to Henry's house. Instead I met up with a paranoid South African and embarked on a three-week hitchhiking odyssey around the countryside. He travelled everywhere with a pair of ice-skates slung around his neck and was convinced people were following him. It seemed quite normal at the time.

My next stop was France, where the carnival came to a grinding halt. It took only a few hours' hitching over the Pyrenees to realise that the balmy weather of Portugal and Spain was not the French standard for this time of year. This became critical at two in the morning about fourteen kilometres outside Perpignan, when I realised that a lift was going to be hard to come by. The snow was coming down, the wind was picking up and I knew I was in trouble.

Out of the night came a car. Gendarmes. But instead offering me a ride into town, they made me stand in the cold while they examined my passport. Satisfied, they pointed the direction to Perpignan and drove off. I was furious, which probably saved my life; I used the energy of my anger to walk through the snowstorm.

To my relief I found a church opening for early-morning Mass and went in to warm up. I stayed there as the congregation flocked in, and by the time the service was over I had recovered. In a café an hour later, I went to pay and discovered my wallet had been stolen. The café owner didn't believe a word of it and took my Leica camera as payment. Knowing he had the better end of the deal, he gave me a couple of hundred francs in change as well. Tired and dispirited, I found a pension and slept, vowing to hate the French for ever. No matter where I was born, France was off the list.

Three months after leaving the *Northern Star*, I eventually made my way to London and set about attempting to earn a living. It did not go well. For a couple of months the nearest I got to the stage was washing dishes in theatre bars. My savings, which had sat in a London bank untouched while I starved in Europe, were sufficient to get me a flat in Earls Court but there were times when, to save money, I made dawn forays to steal bottles of milk from doorsteps. My staple diet for a while was steamed rice with salt as a main and steamed rice with milk and sugar for dessert.

Slowly things began to improve and I found one or two small parts in English repertory theatre. One of the plays was a forgettable farce, the other *The Importance of Being Earnest*. Then Gabrielle arrived.

From the moment she stepped off the ship in Southampton I sensed something was wrong. She greeted me not with open arms but with sullen silence, which persisted for the entire train trip back to London. When I pressed her to explain she refused, and insisted on booking herself into a hostel instead of staying with me. Through friends, I had managed to arrange a job for her at a Thomas Cook travel agency, but the next morning she informed me she was flying back to New Zealand. She handed me an envelope and fled.

In her brief letter, she wrote that she had got drunk on the ship and been seduced by a steward. She was, she claimed, full of remorse and shame at having let me down, and felt it best for all concerned that we never see each other again. Her engagement ring was in the bottom of the envelope. The next morning I flung it in the Thames and in a suicidal depression went back to my flat and turned on the gas. I guess I owe my life to the fact that I hadn't put enough money in the gas meter, and I survived with nothing more than a nauseating headache.

The emotional ache lasted a lot longer, but once I recovered somewhat, England in the 1960s was liberating. Every interesting person on the planet seemed to be in London then. It was a world unto itself and I was surrounded by exciting new music, poetry and ideas without boundaries. One night, sitting in a coffee bar with people from Argentina, the Seychelles, Germany, Sweden, Poland and Israel, I had a moment when I felt that there was nothing we could not achieve. Such idealism might seem naïve viewed from today's economic-rationalist dystopia, but at the time, throwing off the shackles of my antipodean claustrophobia, I found it exhilarating. All the same, part of me was metaphorically checking over my shoulder, afraid that at any moment one of the McCutcheons would grab me by the ear and drag me back to my senses.

Once I got used to London's employment scene, I found non-acting work easy enough to come by and I was able to finance several trips to Europe to hunt for clues to my roots.

I usually went for a month at a time and on each trip I chose a different destination. I concentrated on Germany, Hungary and Czechoslovakia and my modus operandi was always the same. I would spend as much time as possible in train stations, coffee bars, airports, anywhere I could watch people. I was looking for some clue in appearance or language that would spark a memory.

It was of course a quest doomed from the start, but I clung to the notion that somehow or other, with enough force of will, I would stumble upon a pointer to my origins. If Europe was my homeland, then surely some genetic memory would be triggered. I was drawn to notices of missing persons, in police stations and elsewhere. Using phrase books I would painstakingly translate the information on them, and I later spent hours fantasising about the circumstances of these people's disappearances.

It was all good material for my later career as a writer of fiction, but it did little to advance my search. Part of me knew only too well that there was nothing rational about what I was doing, but my hunger for identity on those trips to Europe acknowledged no limitations.

Back in London, though, I gradually came to sense a change taking place. While the search remained important to me, I found it harder and harder to deny its futility, and I was forced to face the fact that I might never know the truth about my background. During those periods when I had nothing to do but think about this, I became depressed. But luckily there was plenty in the city to distract myself with and I dived head first into whatever life served up. Since small theatre parts were impossible to live on, I supplemented them with a diverse range of jobs – copywriting and designing advertisements for an automotive magazine, cataloguing builders' supplies, waiting on tables, selling magazines door to door, and working in the medical-supplies store at St Thomas' Hospital.

The job at St Thomas' was one of the most interesting few months of my life, not because I had a burning desire to know more about rectal catheters, but because of my workmates. The head of the store was an Anglo-Indian with crazy, Marty Feldman eyes. There were three of us working under him, and my two companions were black South Africans who spent most of their time using the repairs workshop to craft pipes and bongs from recycled medical equipment. Their signature piece was a Coke bottle cut in half with the sharp edges ground down, and fitted out with a metal coil in the neck. This was ideal for smoking the hashish they cut into matchbox-size blocks with a hot wire.

We three formed such a close friendship that I ended up moving into their house in Clapham Common, where their mother did marvellous things with hashish and chicken stuffing. Sunday lunch was always hysterically funny.

Our Indian boss paid little attention to anything we underlings did; as long as we turned up, he was happy. He kept the books and took particular care of the parcels that came down the slide from the couriers and delivery vans. For good reason, I discovered. Just before I left to fly back to New Zealand, he was arrested for reselling stolen drugs that the police returned to the hospital. Today, of course, such a crime would be impossible, but these were the heady years of the 1960s and things were much more lax.

Going home was not something that had been on my agenda, but I'd received an offer too good to turn down: an invitation to join New Zealand's first professional theatre company. This was to be based in Christchurch and seemed like a splendid vehicle for the return of the prodigal son. In spite of the fact that my only real theatrical credit to date was playing Thomas Walsingham in the wonderfully middle-named Richard Hengist Horne's 1837 drama *The Death of Marlowe*, the theatre planners in New Zealand considered me employable.

It occurs to me now that this says more about the dearth of talent in New Zealand at the time than about any talent of mine, and it's a mystery that anyone in Christchurch even knew how to contact me. Despite exhaustive research, I can find no trace of a critique of my appearance on the English stage, nor of the production or the company involved. How any of the theatre mavens in New Zealand knew about it remains equally baffling. Back then, though, this was the least of my concerns, and so as not to allow time for anyone to change their mind, I hastily booked a flight to New Zealand, some two years after I'd left.

The week before I flew out, an Irish woman I'd met more than a year previously tracked me down. I'd been quite taken with Margaret Cleary but I'd always kept a respectable distance. Her Catholicism reminded me too much of Gabrielle and our relationship remained chaste. But a year-and-a-half on, the pain of Gabrielle had subsided, and so too had Margaret's Catholic inhibitions. We spent a memorable week together in April 1967, at the end of which we said our fond farewells and I boarded my plane back to New Zealand.

I had high hopes that success with the fledgling Canterbury Theatre Company would open my parents' hearts, change their minds about my creative pursuits, but it was not to be. My return proved as ill-fated as the theatre company. Ignoring the initial fanfare over Christchurch hosting New Zealand's inaugural professional theatre, Mac and Mary did not attend a single show. I was particularly disappointed in my father. He of all people, I thought, with his artistic bent, should have supported my ambition, but on the company's opening night he went to Akaroa for the weekend.

Within less than a year the Canterbury Theatre Company was disbanded and all funding from the Queen Elizabeth II Arts Council was withdrawn. There was some murmuring (rightly, I felt) about the fact that we had done no New Zealand plays and only had a couple of Kiwis in the company. It was an ignominious end to New Zealand's first professional theatre group.

In January 1968, not long before the company split up, I received a letter from Margaret Cleary with the news that she had given birth to our daughter. My shock was such that it was a good few minutes before I was able to read the rest of her letter. She wrote that she had returned to Ireland and was extremely happy to have a child, whom she'd named Chantelle Noelle – for having been born so close to Christmas. Margaret stated in the clearest of terms that she did not expect anything at all from me.

This struck me as both unfair and unusual, and I wrote back saying I would be only too happy to help her come to New Zealand where I'd take care of the two of them. I got no reply, to either that or my subsequent letters. After a while I stopped writing and accepted the inevitable.

Following the demise of my acting career I tried my hand at a variety of things, from teaching theatre skills to running a small restaurant in the town of Blenheim, in the South Island's Marlborough region. It was there in 1968, at the age of twenty-one, that I got married for the first time.

Maryann Montgomery was a nurse at the Marlborough hospital. My engagement to her was not well received by the McCutcheons, but despite expressing the opinion that

'I didn't know what I was doing', they warmed to Maryann when I took her to Christchurch to meet them, and made her feel welcome.

Our marriage did not get off to a good start. Literally. The car we were travelling in to our honeymoon managed just eighty miles before blowing up. When we did finally make it to the family holiday house in Akaroa we succeeded in setting the place on fire. We had been sitting in front of the blazing fireplace when smoke began to drift up through the floor. I rushed down to the dental surgery in the basement to discover that the heat from the fire had ignited the floor joists and a couple of books hidden up in the surgery ceiling. I quickly extinguished the smouldering logs and retrieved the books. The copy of the Kama Sutra had only slight water damage. When I later returned it to Mac he swore he had no idea how it got to be in the ceiling in the first place.

Maryann and I settled down in Christchurch, and after a failed attempt at selling life insurance my prospects looked bleak. All I wanted to do was write and act, but neither occupation offered much financial security. Then Maryann became pregnant and finding a real job became a serious matter.

Unexpectedly I was offered a position in the airline industry, and there followed an exciting stint as a flight purser with Mount Cook Airlines. Based first in Christchurch and later in Queenstown, the job consisted of everything from baggage handling to computing the take-off weight of the aircraft. Flying around the country with tourists in a Douglas Dakota DC3 aircraft was fun for a while, and certainly had its moments.

Once, after a seagull smashed through into the cockpit, we were grounded at the tiny hamlet of Te Anau in the deep south until a new windscreen could be flown in. Other incidents were more serious. A sudden white-out as we were crossing an alpine pass forced us to fly in tight circles until the blizzard passed. The glimpses of ice-covered rock just off the wing tips was disconcerting, to say the least.

It seemed to me that my life expectancy would be enhanced by a career on terra firma, so when the opportunity to audition for a position with the New Zealand Broadcasting Corporation came up, I decided to give it a shot.

Radio was not a career I had ever envisaged for myself, even though I used to spend hours listening to our old valve radio in the cottage at Arthurs Pass. I loved the serials and, strangely, I liked listening to static. High in the mountains I would scan the shortwave bands, pausing for a moment on a gabble of foreign language. Moving on, I discovered frequencies where the broadcast sounded like waves of bombers. Weird sounds, white noise, phasing and echo ran around my skull, painting a million pictures. For a child with an imagination, it was heaven.

The training provided by the NZBC at that time was the best there was, and those who graduated were assured of being employable anywhere in the English-speaking world. Modern media students would find the level of instruction that trainees underwent back then extraordinary.

Prospective broadcasters first had to pass an audition proving they had the ability to read fluently in a well-modulated voice, and many applicants were knocked out at this stage. Those whose voices were judged acceptable were flown to Wellington and accommodated in a government hostel for six to eight weeks of intensive study. Several more of the intake were culled during this period as the demands made upon us increased. We were drilled not only in news-reading, interviewing techniques and general presentation skills, but also in linguistics.

It might seem bizarre now, but we were expected to be able to read in German, French, Italian and Maori. This wasn't about being fluent in those languages —we read from phonetic scripts and had to sit exams in writing and reading such pieces. The aim was to produce broadcasters who could present classical-music programs, for example, without stuttering over the names of composers or performers. Or current-affairs presenters who could eloquently pronounce the names of world leaders. And it worked. Within six weeks we were all happily going through the alphabet from Albrechtsberger and Arensky to Zumsteeg and Zwilich.

I graduated from the training course and was posted to the North Island town of Tauranga as a probationary broadcaster.

For most of the time I was there, no call was made on the skills I had acquired at training school. I was chiefly doing continuity broadcasting – providing the links between music and other segments – along with the occasional interview. I worked various shifts; I used to enjoy working at night but more often than not was rostered on what was quaintly referred to as the 'morning women's program'.

While work was less than challenging, Maryann and I were happy. Our first child was born in 1969 and we named him Guy Maitland, after my best friend Guy Hargreaves and, in what I hoped would be a conciliatory gesture, after Mac (Hugh Maitland) McCutcheon. The McCutcheons appeared to be chuffed at the time, or so Maryann told me; I hadn't seen them since my wedding. Things between us had got so bad that by the time Guy was born, Maryann was my only link to the McCutcheons. My relationship with Mac was particularly bad; he still felt that I had let the family down by not following an academic or professional career. He was unwavering in his belief that I was throwing my life away. In some respects ours was a typical intergenerational conflict, but it was exacerbated by the tension surrounding my adoption.

But being married had given me the nearest thing to a family for the very first time, and despite being estranged from my adoptive family, I remember that period as one of relative emotional stability.

Once my probationary period ended I was posted to

Nelson in the South Island. It was an idyllic town and it seemed that nothing could spoil our happiness. Our second child, Cathryn, was born two years after Guy and was a beautiful girl with the sweetest temperament. Everything was falling into place. I had a decent income and a great circle of interesting friends. Life was good. Too good to last, as it turned out.

Several years earlier, in May 1965, New Zealand had finally caved in to pressure from the United States to commit troops to the war in Vietnam. New Zealand's prime minister, Keith Holyoake, was sceptical of American and Australian claims that the war could be won, and strived to limit the country's involvement. The initial deployment was a mere four-gun artillery battery comprising a hundred and twenty men.

Although New Zealand's contribution to the war was never great in terms of personnel numbers, its effect on the New Zealand public was enormous, and in the late 1960s it was to change the direction of my life completely. The new political consciousness growing out of various social movements – the anti-apartheid movement, the women's movement and Maori rights – began to come together around the issue of New Zealand's involvement in Vietnam. Unlike the anti-war movements in Australia and the United States, the New Zealand reaction sprang not from a reaction to conscription but from a deeply felt and self-consciously nationalistic critique of post-war security policies. The coalition of forces opposing the war drew on everything from pacifist rhetoric and arguments ridiculing the Asian domino theory to the far left's unquestioning support for the communist regime in North Vietnam. There was no united voice on the issue.

In late 1969 a friend and I discerned a need for an underground newspaper to support and bring together these diverse voices. It was a grandiose idea and an impossible task, and what resulted was more satirical and anarchic than even we had intended. *Dag* was not so much a voice as a long, low, throaty chuckle. Naming the newspaper after the little bits of dried dung on a sheep's bum seemed to us perfect.

There was a law in force at the time stipulating that a copy of all publications be lodged with the National Archives. Of course we intended to do no such thing, and in the spirit of the times our first issue was *Dag* Vol. 1, No. 13. This was followed by *Dag* Vol. 2, No. 3, a tactic aimed at keeping the authorities guessing. But the authorities were less than amused by our efforts, and after threatening to close down our friendly printer, they began a harassment of a more personal kind. At first this took the form of messing around with the newspaper's mail, so that articles and artwork from contributors – the Underground Press Syndicate, the Free Press Movement, and others – arrived very late, damaged, or not at all. In those heady, hippie days it all seemed like a grand game of cat-and-mouse, and we derived a lot of pleasure from managing to get each issue out.

Then things turned sour. It became evident that the Security Service thought we were a real threat, although to this day I can not imagine what influence they thought our little rag with a print run of just under five thousand had. The network of people who distributed it free of charge were unknown to each other, and anything less like a coherent organisation is hard to imagine. It was amateur and it was fun.

I knew we were in trouble when I arrived home one night to learn we might all be arrested, or so the neighbours had reported to Maryann. The rumour obviously had her worried, and she angrily announced that my involvement with the newspaper was threatening our marriage. This came as a surprise to me, since up to that point our political views had coincided. They certainly didn't seem to now. According to Maryann, our neighbours had been visited by men in trench coats and informed that we were 'subversive' people. It all felt like a parody gone wrong. I laughed it off, but as I was soon to find out, Maryann had been seriously intimidated.

Several days later, I returned from work to find her in a dreadful state. I don't know if this was a result of the cumulative effects of psychological stress or something else. Her brother Ross was visiting and he was clearly agitated as well. My suggestion that a couple of glasses of orange juice and a quiet chat might be the best way forward garnered no support. Ross, who had just enlisted in the army, accused me of being insane and making his sister's life 'fucking hell'. To add to the strength of his assertion he produced an old bayonet, with which he proceeded to stab at the air.

Then things took a comic turn. This is one image which is as clear in my mind as a photograph: Maryann on the stairs with Cathryn in her arms; in front of her Ross with the bayonet. I retreated behind the coffee table and sat down, hoping his anger would subside. Then he produced a hand grenade.

Now, I am usually pretty unflappable but I have to admit I was unnerved. And more so when he pulled the pin. Ross threw the grenade at me and I did what anyone who'd watched enough old movies would have done. I caught it. But clumsily, and it hit me on the temple. It was of course only a dummy practice grenade; nevertheless it was heavy and the top edge gave me a nasty gash.

For a few minutes I sat while the blood ran down my face, until I realised the cut needed treating.

'Don't come back, bastard!' Ross called after me as I left the house.

'Well, dear, what have we done to ourselves?' the night nurse asked.

'Got hit on the head with a hand grenade,' I replied. I would have blushed if I'd had blood to spare.

'Tch, tch,' she said. 'Boys will be boys.'

Things went downhill from there. After spending the night at a friend's place, I went home willing to forgive and forget – as long as Ross went to Vietnam and Maryann was prepared to acknowledge the ridiculousness of the notion that my protesting the war made me a danger to society. But there was nobody home. Maryann had vanished with the children and I found myself under surveillance even at work. The Security Service had informed the NZBC that I intended to use the airwaves for an anti-war tirade, and had positioned someone to observe me while I worked. Of course I had never had any such intention. The situation was out of control, so I resigned.

I never discovered where Maryann went for those weeks. At the time I assumed she'd gone to stay with her parents, but they wouldn't admit as much to me when I called. My career with the NZBC being over, I desperately needed work and so I left Nelson and took the only alternative radio job in New Zealand at the time, with a private radio station in Hamilton, in the North Island's Waikato district.

The two years I spent in Hamilton were rewarding from a career point of view. My radio programs were well regarded, and the experience I gained in interviewing and presenting a night-time music show were to stand me in good stead in years to come. But while my life was fine on the surface, underneath I was a mess. I missed my children dreadfully, and to make matters worse the three Marys in my life were set against me; Mary McCutcheon and Mary Jane had sided with Maryann. I was bluntly informed that I was no longer part of either family. Once Maryann and I had come to an agreement on maintenance payments, I had no contact at all with her or with my children. Mary McCutcheon did not reply to my letters and refused to divulge Maryann's new address.

Needless to say, the effect on me was devastating. It reopened the wounds from my childhood and compounded my growing feeling of despair. Somehow, though, I managed to react not with anger or depression but with a newfound feeling that if this was the way the world operated then I would try to alter it. The change brought by seeing things this way was liberating and I determined to make a new beginning. Ever since childhood, I had been attempting to fit myself into a mould that denied the reality of who I was. While I was no closer to discovering my true identity, I knew with absolute certainty that I was not the person so despised by the McCutcheon family. The past could not be eradicated but it could be dismissed.

It was while I was living in Hamilton that Mac McCutcheon died, in 1972. The depth of the schism in our family is evidenced by the fact that I was unaware he was even ill; I wasn't told about his death, nor was I invited to the funeral. That we died estranged has always caused me much remorse: I would give anything for him to see me today and to know how much the success I've had is due to the foundations and education that he and Mary provided me with.

In the face of this rejection by the family I made the decision to convert my anger into action. This harnessing of negative energy and its transformation into something positive was the first step in the right direction I had taken in years.

I've always had a streak of idealism, and I sensed that it was the right time, culturally and politically as well as personally, to set about some serious investigation of alternative ways of living. Nothing I had tried to date had assuaged my deep feelings of alienation, and it seemed to me that I had little to lose by striking out in new directions. Career opportunities in New Zealand were limited and the country felt as though it were home to little more than my failures. This realisation soon led to my decision to leave New Zealand for good.

I moved to Australia in 1973, and not long afterwards a friend told me he thought he'd seen Maryann in Melbourne. I checked the electoral roles, to no avail. I wasn't living in Melbourne but whenever I passed through I would sit on a bench near Flinders Street Station and spend hours watching the faces, hoping to recognise my own children. Hopeful, and yet with fear in the pit of my stomach that I would see them and not know what to do. It was a sad recurrence of my sitting at train stations in Europe, trying to identify my mother tongue.

It's hard even in hindsight to fathom the mentality of those who considered it necessary to 'protect' my wife and children from me, even after I'd left the country. People I had thought of as mutual friends of Maryann and mine dropped me, and Mary McCutcheon maintained her policy of preventing me from making contact with Guy and Cathryn.

My children were, of course, the one family tie I never wanted to cut, and over the years I continued to send them presents for Christmas and birthdays. But I had to do so via Mary McCutcheon. Hers was the only address I had, and I would enclose a letter to her asking for the children's whereabouts. But the answer was always the same: they wanted nothing to do with me. I had attained black-sheep status.

In the late 1970s I received a letter from a lawyer informing me that Maryann had remarried and requesting my agreement to the children's names being changed. I refused. (As it turned out, they had been using their stepfather's surname for some years, but it was a while before I discovered that.)

It was nineteen years before I saw my children again. In January 1991 Guy, who was living in Melbourne with Cathryn, Maryann and her new husband, found some letters from me in one of Maryann's drawers. Mary McCutcheon had forwarded them on and they came, as Guy was later to tell me, as a real shock. He had been raised thinking I was some kind of evil drug dealer in Sydney. At about the same time, *The Age* ran a feature on me to coincide with the première of one of my plays by the Melbourne Theatre Company. Guy wasn't sure I was the same person but he wrote to me anyway.

I was then working for Radio National in Hobart, but the day his letter arrived I was doing an outside broadcast from the University of Western Australia in Perth. As I came off air my producer handed me the letter, which had been forwarded from Hobart. Hand-written on pink paper, it had an extraordinary effect on me. I remember walking around the campus with tears rolling down my cheeks. He'd included a phone number and so, after composing myself, I rang him.

My immediate impression was, of all things, a negative reaction to his strong Australian accent – I felt sad that in the fifteen or so years he'd been living in Melbourne he'd lost his New Zealand vowels. We agreed to meet when I was next in Melbourne, and when we did it was easier than I'd imagined; Guy's open nature made communication easy. And yet I felt as though I were meeting not my son but a stranger who'd been taken away before I could get to know him. There was no welling of fatherly emotions, but rather a sadness that we could never regain the years that had been taken from us.

Guy and I share a lot of the same attributes: an offbeat sense of humour and a relaxed attitude about keeping in touch. A couple of years after we made contact he disappeared for months, and then out of the blue he turned up on my doorstep asking if he could stay for a couple of weeks. I was living alone in a small house and I enjoyed having him around.

Cathryn was more hesitant about meeting me, but eventually we arranged to do so at the end of 1991, at Melbourne's Monash University, where I was to be presented with an Adult Educator of the Year award on behalf of the radio program I was hosting at the time. She was dressed beautifully and looked so much like her mother, but it soon became clear that she had no need of a long-lost father in her life just then. Her own family was real, whereas I was a phantom from the past. For Cathryn I suspect I will always be a stranger, someone to whom she is related but never had the chance to know.

In many ways the chasm between my children and me mirrors my situation with the McCutcheons. My son and daughter were also lied to, and it changed their lives for ever. That we have failed to achieve closeness is tragic, and this doesn't seem destined to change any time soon. But I still have hope that as they mature they will feel the same need to connect that has driven me.

Losing touch with my children is something that, because of my childhood experiences, I think I've been even more affected by than most who find themselves in this situation. I've often felt that it's an unavoidable cycle, one from which I can never break free. When a sense of abandonment and betrayal is etched deeply into the subconscious it tends to have an impact on all subsequent relationships. Right from the beginning, those relationships are built on an almost biological certainty that they will be lost. This not only becomes self-fulfilling but is, as I was later to discover, a common experience for those in similar circumstances.

Only one thing appears to have the potential to break the cycle and that is finding a way to mend the flaws in the original template formed during childhood. For most people this is impossible, and even if they do uncover the truth about their past, their behaviour is often too deeply ingrained to be changed.

For many years I was fortunate to have two beautiful stepdaughters, Rose and Wren, who lived with me from their pre-school days in the 1980s to the beginning of their university years in the early 1990s. I was totally devoted to them. When their mother chose a new partner she made it clear that they too had a choice, but they understandably put their mother's wishes first and ended all contact with me. It was a hurt that did not recede with time. And once again it fed the neurosis that had been set up by my abandonment as a child – if I was not worthy of being loved by my own mother, then I was not worthy of being loved by anyone. It was another rotation in the endless cycle of love and loss.

My second marriage, in the late 1970s, was an altogether happier affair, and Arwen and I have two wonderful children, Maha and Alia, a daughter and son of whom we are immensely proud. Delivering my own son at home and being present at the birth of my daughter was an enormous blessing. My strongest memory of Alia's birth is holding him in my hands and feeling so relieved that he would never have to question who his parents were. As a parent I was far from perfect, but the bonds formed at birth helped forge a very special link with my children.

Arwen and I later parted amicably and we remain friends. Both Maha and Alia followed me to Brisbane, where they set out on career paths close to their hearts. To have my daughter value our friendship enough to insist on weekly meetings for lunch proves to me just how strongly love can overcome even my mediocre parenting skills. Given my inbuilt distrust of relationships, it is to my children and their mother's credit that we have such a good family bond.

Chapter 8

Nineteen kilometres northwest of Hamilton, on a beautiful bend in the Waikato River, lies the little town of Ngaruawahia, the Maori capital of New Zealand and the home of the Maori Queen. In January 1973 it was chosen as the location for New Zealand's first major outdoor rock festival, an event that was to prove another turning point in my life. Its effect was perhaps the stronger for coming during a time of such personal loss – the break-up of my first marriage and family.

I had always loved live music, but before Ngaruawahia I had never had the opportunity to get up close and personal with rock stars. The radio station I worked for was promoting the festival, and in the normal course of events I would have had the usual free tickets in return for plugging it on air. But then I met the festival's co-producer, Robert Raymond, who became a lifelong friend, and with the doors he opened I found myself not only backstage with the fifty-plus acts, but centre stage introducing many of them.

Robert Raymond's vision was for an antipodean Woodstock, and in many ways he and his co-producer succeeded – that is, in every way but financially. The crowds were great but with fifty-four acts to pay, Robert was servicing the debts for several years. Artistically, though, it was a sensation, right from the moment the opening performer, Corben Simpson, romped naked onstage through to Black Sabbath's burning of a cross on the hill at the head of the valley. The music was also pretty damned good. For music buffs, The Great Ngaruawahia Music Festival is noteworthy for being one of the first major appearances of Split Enz and the very first gig by Dragon, albeit without Marc Hunter. Todd Hunter had pulled the band together for the festival and chosen the band's name from the I Ching.

My old friend Bruno Lawrence was one of the hits of the festival with his new band Blerta, an acronym of The Bruno Lawrence Electric Revelation Travelling Apparition. The standout performance for me, though, was the legendry British folk-rock band Fairport Convention. Or to be more accurate, their wonderful lead singer, Sandy Denny. In the heat of the festival I fell madly in love with Boadicea, as the band's fiddler Dave Swarbrick called her. As well as sharing a name, Sandy and I were both born in 1947 and we hit it off from the first moment. It was one of those rare and delightful relationships that was as unstoppable as it was impossible, due to Sandy having to leave the country as soon as the festival was over.

We wrote to each other a couple of times in the next few months, but then the letters stopped and I heard nothing until the following year, when she sent me a copy of her album, *Like an Old Fashioned Waltz*. She had drawn a circle round the last track, 'No End', which to this day remains one of my favourite songs. Inside was a short letter saying that the previous September she had married. Four years later Sandy fell down some stairs and suffered a brain haemorrhage. She lay in a coma for three days before she died, at the age of thirty-one. Despite the fact that we'd only ever spent a few days together, I was devastated.

But those few days of total immersion in rock and folk culture inspired me for life, and to this day I remain involved with live music through Australia's Woodford Festival, a very sophisticated affair compared to Ngaruawahia.

Woodford is like a huge family that gets together for a week-long celebration once a year. The logistics of organising a festival with up to two thousand performers for an audience of around a hundred thousand are daunting, and yet each year director Bill Hauritz and his dedicated team pull it together. Compared to their work, my contribution is minuscule, but it's nevertheless immensely enjoyable. I work on a range of things, from scripting the opening ceremony to dealing with festival guests and sponsors, but the role I most like and look forward to is a simpler one: each year I get behind one of the festival bars and have a great time being an anonymous barman.

It was shortly after the Ngaruawahia festival that I decided to quit New Zealand and try to make a career in Australia. Everything I had heard from friends there suggested a country that was musically miles ahead of New Zealand. A musician friend sent me a tape of a radio show called *Room to Move*, hosted by a broadcaster named Chris Winter. It was a revelation. I found myself listening to literate rock with literate commentary. My own program, *Bed Rock*, was on the surface similar, but after listening to Chris Winter I saw that the difference was stark. He really knew what he was talking about, whereas I was recycling material from magazines and album covers.

Another force driving me out of New Zealand was a weariness with the politics. Although I was sickened by the hypocrisy and double standards I observed in the mainstream, I nevertheless still harboured a deep reservoir of idealism. My early interest in communism had foundered once I learned about Stalin's horrendous crimes. The Great Helmsman, Chairman Mao, was also looking more and more tarnished. Green politics held a definite lure, but being in its infancy seemed incapable of delivering real change in the short term. As for the major parties, they had always struck me as badly separated Siamese twins. What I needed, I decided, was a new start. Fresh fields. Bruno Lawrence, Corben Simpson and Blerta were all heading to Australia. It seemed like a good time for me to leave too.

In many ways Australia felt much like New Zealand, but while Australians were more relaxed and laid back, I found them surprisingly less self-confident. I soon got used to the nasal whine and the injection of swear words into every second sentence. The landscape took more time. Whereas the forests in New Zealand were soft, green and enfolding, the Australian bush felt hard and alienating. It was also full of dangerous wildlife. My first impression was of a harsh dry country whose sheer size mitigated against intimacy. In New Zealand distances were manageable, conceivable.

When I'd informed Radio Waikato that I was leaving, a staff member who coveted my job there very helpfully organised a position for me with a station in Australia where he had contacts. At that time my knowledge of Australia was so rudimentary that when he told me the station was in the far north of Queensland I thought nothing of it. I flew into Brisbane accompanied by my girlfriend at the time and we caught a connecting flight to Cairns.

It did seem like a long way, even at that point, but it wasn't until we hired a car and set out to drive to Mareeba that I began to have doubts about the wisdom of the venture. To make matters worse, I discovered that the letter of offer I'd received on the station's letterhead had not been written by them, and there was in fact no opening.

We booked into the local pub, where we were entertained by yarns from the town's policeman about the ongoing violence between the area's Serbs and Croats. The next morning we were back in the car heading for Townsville. Fortunately both of the radio stations there offered me work on air and my girlfriend a position as a copywriter. After listening to the music mix of each station, we settled for Radio 4TO.

Townsville in the 1970s was an interesting place, an army town with a deeply entrenched conservatism. Yet the young people were welcoming and we soon warmed to the laissez-faire attitude, and I found that I was forgiven my trans-Tasman vowels. The year I spent there was not entirely trouble-free, as the station management took a dim view of my predilection for playing music which they considered to be outside of the mainstream. My late-night airing, without a break, of Jeannie Lewis's now classic first album, *Free Fall Through Featherless Flight,* came close to getting me fired.

I managed to redeem myself somewhat by organising an outdoor concert by the then immensely popular Brian Cadd, although management were less than impressed when they discovered that Brian, one of his backing singers and I had broadcast a rather drunken rendition of 'Ginger Man' live to air from the station's radio car at three in the morning. Shortly afterwards they facilitated my transfer to a sister station in

Launceston. My girlfriend, to my disappointment, opted to remain in Townsville.

On moving to Tasmania I purchased a farm on a small piece of land in the mountains of the northwest, and in order to be closer to it I changed jobs and moved to the town of Devonport, an hour-and-a-half's drive away. When I first discovered this remote valley of Lorinna I knew instantly that it was the place where I could fulfil my desire to adopt a different lifestyle. The hippie era seemed to have bypassed Tasmania, but the locals soon adopted me as a variety of the species.

The valley was in an ideal setting, at an altitude of some three hundred metres, and the property was nestled in the folds of the forest on the shores of Lake Cethana. Without interference from electric lights, the stars burned fiercely, reminding me of nights in the mountains of New Zealand.

Being so far from the nearest town, I soon had to expand my notions of setting up a community to include the necessity of being self-sufficient. This was an exciting challenge, but one that required more than my meagre capital, and so for the first year I spent three hours a day commuting to Devonport. As the scope of my undertaking expanded so did the need for funds, and I quit my job in Devonport and headed to Sydney, where I spent an amazing year working for Double Jay, the precursor of Triple Jay.

Double Jay was a great leap forward for the radio industry and for its audience. It was alternative, socialist, ready to push the boundaries and break the rules. From day one of transmission it threw down the gauntlet, its first piece of music being the opening track from Skyhooks' *Living in the 70s* – 'You Just Like Me 'Cos I'm Good in Bed'. That, along with the openly dope-inspired slogan, 'The Head of the Dial', left nobody in doubt that change was in the air – if not already on the air.

The wowsers predictably came out in force, and I remember the pride I felt when Reverend Fred Nile described me in a newspaper column as 'being possessed by the devil'.

Having the chance to work with people like Chris Winter, Lex Marinos, Mac Cocker, Marius Web and Gayle Austin was a real privilege, and yet I was restless to get back to Tasmania. Like many of my contemporaries, I was doing my fair share of spiritual supermarket shopping, and then one day I had the good fortune to interview Anne McNeil, a Tibetan nun. Something strange happened in that interview. In the small recording booth she looked me straight in the eye and asked me if I understood that enlightenment was achievable within a single lifetime.

'It is the experience of being silent and innocent, of being full of wonder and awe,' she said. And then added, 'Go back to your farm and live the life of Marpa.'

It was a Saul-on-the-road-to-Damascus experience. Over the following weeks I read biographies of Marpa, the eleventh-century translator who brought the Buddha's teachings to

Tibet, and of his most famous pupil, Milarepa. By the time I'd worked my way through *The One Hundred Thousand Songs of Milarepa* I was ready to return to Tasmania.

For me Tibetan Buddhism was a natural fit, its wonderfully optimistic stories the antithesis of the thundering Christian monologues I had grown up with. The Mahayana school of Buddhism teaches that the focus of practice should be on compassion. This made perfect sense to me and I discovered that the more I turned my attention to the suffering of others, the less intense my own neuroses felt. The longing to know my roots was not gone completely, but in the grand scheme of things it felt insignificant. Convinced that the world did not have to be the way it was, I decided that even if I couldn't change it, at least I could provide an antidote to its more poisonous aspects.

In late 1975 I left Sydney and went back to the farm. Shortly afterwards my girlfriend and co-worker at Double Jay, Jenny West, arrived with her young son Craig. Jenny, who shared my interest in Tibetan Buddhism, changed her name to the Tolkien-inspired Arwen and became a founding member of what was to develop into the Illusion Farm Retreat Centre. A year later our son Alia was born in the little cottage on the farm, and not long after that I made a flying visit to the Buddhist centre at Eudlo in Queensland, where I had the great good fortune to meet my future teacher, Lama Zasep Tulku. On his instructions I returned to Tasmania fired by the promise that if I built a meditation hall he would come and give teachings.

What followed proved to be a victory of enthusiasm over experience. In the space of about six months and on a tiny budget, we constructed a large meditation hall, or gompa, and shortly afterwards we commenced work on a kitchen and dormitory complex, as well as several huts. At each step of the way people with the necessary skill materialised. Possibly this was due to word of our strange enterprise spreading, but Buddhists would say it was simply good karma.

One of the most extraordinary individuals who assisted us was a man named Harold Riley, a logger from the small rural community of Sheffield, which was an hour's drive from the farm. Over the years I'd had periods of no income, or periods when I needed to find extra money to keep the farm going, and Harold had been kind enough to give me work from time to time carting hay. When he heard about the building we were doing he offered to help.

Along with his bush skills, Harold brought with him his other great love – a bullock team. The day we walked the team out of Sheffield, over the top of Mt Roland and down into the valley remains one of my most treasured memories. Ambling along at bullock-pace, Harold was able to point out things about the countryside that I had never seen in all my hundreds of car trips.

At the time I had a beautiful Clydesdale mare named Tai, who did all the ploughing on the farm. Between Tai and the bullocks we were able to extract all the logs required for the gompa without damaging the surrounding bush. The construction was a log hexagon, with each of the six-metre, two-tonne logs slowly rolled into place by the gently coaxed bullock team. The roofing was more problematic. In keeping with the design and location, we settled on shingles, but having never split a shingle in my life I found it a daunting prospect. Harold, ever patient, promised to teach me once we found a tree with suitable wood.

This took six weeks. Shingles need to be made from wood that will split easily, and the only candidate we could find was miles away and required sawing into lengths for transportation. But once you have the wood, the ancient art of making shingles is a rewarding, if exhausting, task. Together Harold and I split the required eight and a half thousand shingles in four days, and the end result was well worth the effort.

The entire gompa was built without a single plan being drawn on paper and by the time it was completed, Arwen and I had been joined by a wonderful group of young people. Together we set about the task of providing a place where anyone with problems could come to get their life in order. Our volunteers were from all parts of Australia, some who'd come with problems of their own and then stayed on to help others, some who were simply inspired to join in the building of a community. Over time they constructed a variety of dwellings for themselves, ranging from mud-brick cottages to simple wooden huts. The philosophy of the farm was simple.

Our Buddhism was not to be focused on esoteric practices, but rather on providing refuge to 'whoever came up the drive', as we used to put it.

In 1979 Arwen and I were approached by Labor Senator Michael Tate to sponsor a Sri Lankan monk who was seeking asylum. 'You'd need to be married, though,' he informed us. Arwen and I had no hesitation and were married in Devonport a few weeks later.

The number of long-term residents at Illusion Farm fluctuated, but usually hovered around nine to fifteen. The number of casual visitors – those who remained a day or so – was staggering, and over the years would have numbered in the thousands. Our once-a-year meditation courses drew about eighty people. But it was the energy and compassion of our regular group that, for almost a decade, enabled the farm to provide so many people with a new start. It was also due to two great teachers of 'crazy wisdom'.

The first was the lama I met in Queensland in 1976, Zasep Tulku Rinpoche, my teacher and friend, whose teachings on compassion have been at the centre of my life ever since. The second was yet another of the men named Guy who have figured so prominently in my life. This Guy was my companion on the inner journey, Guy Turnbull, a man who embodied compassion. Guy and Zasep remain an inspiration on a path I stumble along to this day.

For many of the so-called 'baby-boomer Buddhists' the

dharma, or Buddhist law, was about accumulating teachings, initiations and 'lama grasping'. For us Illusion Farmers it was about dharma in practice. It was about putting others first. The most beautiful and yet simple example I saw of this came from a young woman named Chrissie. One winter's night at around three in the morning, I heard a car coming up the valley towards the farm. I pulled on some clothes and a pair of gumboots and headed out the door, intending to go and stoke the fire in the communal dining room. It was wet and misty and cold, and there, coming across the paddock in a nightie, holding a kerosene light, was Chrissie.

'There are people coming,' she said. 'I thought they might be hungry.'

That, to me, is a simple yet perfect example of the true spirit of Buddhism.

Illusion Farm was also the place where I was able to apply myself fully to writing for the first time, and where I wrote the majority of my plays. Feeling centred and content allowed my creativity to flourish. The acting talents of the farm members brought my plays to life and took us on a journey which changed us all. For a few brief years the Illusion Circus Theatre Company toured around Tasmania and then interstate. Between productions we would return to our hidden valley and recharge our batteries.

Things could not get much better than this, I thought at the time. I was wrong. Things would get even better, but there was a rough road to travel first.

Eventually things changed. Arwen and I agreed to go our different ways. When opportunities for my plays began to open up I used this as a means of once again changing direction. As the idealism of the 1970s began to fade in the glare of the more self-centred and pragmatic 1980s, I left the farm and merged back into the outside world. But the hard work and dedication of the original farm members is something that has stayed with me as a source of inspiration, as has the invigoration of living in such idyllic natural surroundings while contributing to something so fundamentally worthwhile. It was there too that for the second time in my life I felt as if I belonged to a real family.

There is a less than happy postscript to the story of Illusion Farm. I went overseas for a couple of years and Arwen chose to stay on, with the property deed remaining in my name. On my return to Tasmania it was evident that things would be administratively simpler if Arwen's name were on the papers, and so I 'sold' the farm to her for a dollar. When the time came for Arwen to leave the farm herself, she sold all but a small piece of the property to a fellow member.

By this stage, the style and nature of the farm had changed radically and it was being run more or less as a business. People were now charged a fee to visit, something which was an anathema to me and to the spirit in which the place had been founded. The stories I heard from ex-members suggested that while Illusion Farm might still be serving a useful purpose for a different set of people, it was not the purpose for which I and others had worked so hard.

In 2001 some of the original Illusion Farm members got to together and attempted to buy the farm back, with a view to restoring its original direction. But so much had things changed that what once had been guided by communal spirit now required a committee, and what I had intended as a gift eventually ended up costing a great deal of money. The original members had to fundraise to meet the price of the farm, and in one darkly comic moment I found myself in receipt of a letter asking me to make a donation in order to buy back the land and buildings I had given away for nothing.

Years before, His Holiness the Dalai Lama had written that we should join no associations, but simply practise the dharma as they had in Tibet. These days, much of Buddhism *is* an association.

In the end, Illusion Farm was a wonderful test of non-attachment, which I dealt with in my own imperfect way. The practice of compassion is not dependent on place or people, but on what comes in front of you. And the wonderful friendships that I formed there are a rich and ongoing part of my life that I count as a blessing.

In 1981, while I was still living on Illusion Farm, the government of Finland sponsored a Canberra production of one of my plays, *From the Absence of Sunshine*, which was based on the Finnish epic poem the Kalevala.

There had been nothing premeditated about my excursion into things Finnish, whatever forgotten influences from my grandfather may have been at work in my subconscious. After exploring the harrowing events of wartime Poland in my play *The Truce*, I was in need of a completely different experience. A passing reference to the Kalevala in something I was reading took me in search of it, and undaunted by its 20 000-odd lines of verse, I became fixated on the idea of adapting it for the stage. But whereas *The Truce* had been a tight, three-actor piece in precise historical context, the Kalevala demanded an epic approach for its world of myth and magic.

I completed the play, and when it went into production in Devonport I wrote to the Finnish Embassy in Canberra and asked if they could supply some posters of Finland to display in the foyer of the theatre. They went one better; they not only sent the posters but also despatched the cultural attaché, Ilkka Heiskanen, to attend the opening night.

The Kalevala is drummed into Finns at school in the same manner Shakespeare is in the English-speaking world and, as he later confessed to me, Ilkka Heiskanen was anticipating a dull evening. Nothing had prepared him for our production, which was stripped back to its pagan roots.

Ilkka's delighted reaction resulted in a generous grant for a performance of the play in Canberra, and eventually to my being awarded the Kalevala Medal, for services to Finnish culture. I still treasure a beautiful edition of the great Finnish novel *Seven Brothers*, by Alekis Kivi, which Ilkka sent to me inscribed, 'To Sandy, the eighth brother of Finnish culture'.

From the Absence of Sunshine was the first step in a journey that took me to Finland for a couple of years, initially on a Finnish government scholarship organised by the embassy in Canberra, and later as a broadcaster.

I was just finalising my trip when I received a telegram from my London agent saying he'd sold *The Truce*. There was to be a West End production starring Vanessa Redgrave and Francis de la Tour, my agent told me, so would I like to come to London for discussions and a possible rewrite of the script? It wasn't the sort of offer anyone was likely to refuse.

I reorganised my travel plans and within a couple of weeks found myself in an alien world. My agent and the producers of the play had arranged for me to stay in a beautiful old cottage belonging to Roger Smith, who had recently produced the very successful *Steaming*. My instructions were simple: rewrite the play to toughen up Ms Redgrave's part. I had six weeks in which to get everything done, after which I needed to be in Finland to take up my scholarship.

Once I'd completed the rewrite I returned to London to watch Frances de la Tour in a production of Eugene O'Neill's

A Moon for the Misbegotten. Within five minutes of seeing her on stage I knew her casting alongside Redgrave was perfect.

After that things moved fast. I spun through a whirlwind of meetings, script-readings, trans-Atlantic phone conferences, and already there was talk of following the West End season with a New York production, where Frances de la Tour's part would be taken by Vanessa's sister Lynn. This was to be the first time they'd worked together on stage. My agent was also negotiating with the company Home Box Office for a telemovie of the play. It was all heady stuff for me after life on Illusion Farm.

Then it was time to leave for Finland, and shortly afterwards a Christmas card arrived from my agent – and the whole dream evaporated. Tucked away in a postscript was a note that the production was off because Vanessa had been called away to attend a court case in the United States. The play's financial backers were sure to mount the production at a later date, my agent reassured me, but by the time Vanessa was free again the backers and their money had moved on.

Needless to say, the news did not make for a good Christmas, but I got over my disappointment and settled into my cottage in the forest some thirty miles north of the Finnish capital. This was to be my home for the next two years, and here I found that the space and time was right to examine my past through writing. Although all my plays had to some extent been about the notion of identity, I had never directly attempted to force my inner demons onto the page. In Finland, there was something about the isolation – geographic, linguistic and climatic – that turned me back on myself, particularly during the snowed-in weeks of the year. In the beginning I thought it was merely the presence of something I'd loved so much as a child – snow – but the more I thought about it, the more I came to believe that it was the isolation, the distance from anything familiar, that was working on my psyche.

When I first moved into the cottage a wave of depression washed over me and I became convinced that every one of my real family was dead. I was the last survivor. There was an empty space where my memories should have been and I longed to plunge into it – not to discover, but to be lost. For only the third time in my life I felt a desire for oblivion, for death. The first time, back in the alps in New Zealand, had been because of a state of rapture so complete that nothing more seemed worth having. The second was when Gabrielle left me in London. Here in Finland it was because I felt drained of all hope.

Yet on the bedrock of my despair I laid a foundation. I did what I had always done and turned to fiction. Since the age of nine or ten I had been writing stories and poetry, and I had long ago learned that I wrote best in moments of sadness or doubt. Now, in that bleak space, I began to construct an imaginary cottage. It was small, compact and self-contained.

I took a long time building it. Like many houses, it was not a home, it was a trap. A lure.

In writing *Talvi Maja* (*Winter Cottage*) I created the conditions to raise old ghosts. It was safe, I told myself; it was fiction. It was a literary hoax perpetrated on myself, and it worked. Slowly the memories began to return – of my paternal grandfather, my early schooldays, my childhood loves, Mac and Mary McCutcheon and Mary Jane. I grieved for them all. Having so much come flooding back while writing was unnerving, but it was a valuable lesson in how even the most deeply buried and suppressed memories can rise up spontaneously. The past, I realised, was not dead, it was merely asleep. Yet the secrets surrounding my birth, my first few years and my real family remained hidden from me.

Once the memories of my grandfather had retreated, I kept searching. I let my writing go wherever it desired, and was rewarded with the image of a magician. I have no idea where this image came from, and it was one that never returned, but given what I was later to discover about my birth family, it seems to me extraordinary. Here is an extract from *Talvi Maja*:

> In the attic of my cottage is a trunk. In the trunk is a magician's cape. I know I must dig through the trunk until I find it. It is my real father's cape – perhaps.
> Had he been a magician? Did he pull rabbits out of

hats? Cut women in half? He was certainly good at vanishing. He'd vanished for my entire life.

 I climb the stairs to the attic. The top stairs are dusty, the boards creak. I struggle to push the trapdoor up. Then with a heave it is open and I clamber up into a long room illuminated by a single shaft from a skylight. Cobwebs. Of course there would be cobwebs. Old ones, trailing like lace in the still air. A rocking-horse, broken furniture, cabin trunks with the labels faded and peeling.

 I tiptoe forward and examine them. The labels bear the names of places far distant, redolent with the promise of forbidden adventure. Luxor. Khartoum, Agra, Crete, Santiago . . . There are locks on the trunks. Locks whose keys have long been lost, placed for safekeeping in intricately carved boxes that are later misplaced themselves. These are adventures that can never be revisited.

 On hands and knees I move to the middle of the attic. Draped over a hatstand is a moth-eaten army greatcoat. On the floor a shoebox tied with string so old it disintegrates at my touch. Inside the box are photographs. 'For the family album' says a handwritten note. But the photographs have faded into a uniform sepia in which nothing is distinguishable.

Further in now. At the far end of the attic, where the shadows are longest and the mantilla of cobwebs thickest, is the magician's trunk. It is easy to recognise. The blue satin covering is decorated with glittering stars and half-moons. To my relief there is no lock here. I lift the lid and prop it open.

The first thing I see is the cape, deep purple and hooded. I lift it out and slip my arms into sleeves that are far too big for me. It dwarfs me, and my feet disappear under long folds of cloth. Yet for a moment there is magic. I feel myself grow more solid and I reach back into the trunk. I will find a wand in here. I will make him reappear and . . .

And what? Will I ask him to explain? No, I don't think so. I just want to see my father's tricks.

Knowing that whatever I wrote was safe from critique by anyone, that there was no possibility of being exposed, gave me the freedom to pry open long-locked doors; to write words like 'mother' and 'father' without hiding the tears they evoked. Men carry a cruel burden in not being able to cry without feeling shame. This is a feature of the majority of cultures around the world, but for what reason? Is there any evolutionary justification for it? Not that I can see. But it mattered little what I thought about the sociology of male tears, because they flowed involuntarily along with the memories.

As befits a novel based on such self-centred introspection, *Talvi Maja* was never published. Yet of all the things I've written it remains one of my favourites.

It was also while I was living in Finland that I returned to writing poetry for the first time in many years, drawing heavily on the feelings of alienation and sadness I had long denied. It had become clear to me that no matter how busy I kept myself, the question of my identity was one that was going to haunt me all my life. The clock was ticking, and with every year that went by it became more and more likely that my real parents were dead. That they had not been looking for me I took as further evidence that this was true. Surely, I convinced myself, if they were alive they would come looking.

Whenever I allowed my feelings to overwhelm me – something which at this time I had trouble avoiding – it was invariably the thought of my mother that was paramount. For some reason my father was never an issue. Did my mother know where I was? What language did she speak? Had she died when I was young or had we been torn apart? The idea that she could have given me up voluntarily did not enter my mind. My adoption, I told myself, must have been caused by a traumatic event.

During this period I had horrific dreams in which my mother was dragged away from me, or I from her. In the dreams she would sob as she vanished into an indescribable blackness. There was always a blow to my head that caused me to lose consciousness, and when I awoke it was to find myself alone and hungry. Crying. In light of what I would learn many years later, it is telling that I was only two or three years old in these dreams.

When my year-long scholarship was up I stayed on in Finland to work with the Finnish Broadcasting Corporation, reading the English-language news for the overseas service. My time in that country remains one of the highlights of my life. It wasn't just the sheer beauty of the countryside, with its myriad lakes and islands, that enchanted me, but also the people and culture. At close range, the ostensibly taciturn and almost obsessively shy nature of the Finns melted like snow in spring, and revealed a warm and welcoming people with a dogged determination to overcome the barriers that geography, history and language had set at their door.

The linguistic barrier is immense. Few languages rival Finnish in complexity, and with its Finno-Ugric roots it is alien to most European ears. This was something that, on my part, even study did little to improve. When I arrived in Finland I enrolled in a diploma in Finnish at Helsinki University, for which I studied part-time while writing. I commuted between the cottage and the city by bus and tram, and on the day I received my diploma I was on my way home on the tram when the man next to me addressed me in Finnish. I understood nothing at all of what he said. Eventually, frustrated by my lack of response, he asked me in English if I would please let him get off the tram. So much for my diploma.

From then on I picked up my Finnish from the children I babysat for the locals near my cottage. My accent was perfect and my pronunciation was flawless – thanks to my training as an actor and at the NZBC – but I had the vocabulary of a six-year-old. As one friend kindly explained, 'People think you're Finnish, but they're sorry you've suffered some form of brain damage.'

Three words capture my Finnish experience: SAD, sauna and *sisu*. The climate, with its short summers, gloomy autumns and spectacular winters and springs, can appear exotic to an outsider: the endless summer days when the sun hardly sets before it rises again, and long days and nights of mid-winter darkness with only the briefest period of sunlight. To many Finns, however, this is a recipe for Seasonal Affective Disorder, or SAD as it is appropriately acronymed. The symptoms of SAD were first recorded as long ago as 1845, although it wasn't officially named until the 1980s, and are a result of the extreme variations of seasonal light in Finland, which affects human circadian rhythms.

The approach of autumn was accompanied by a marked change in many of my Finnish friends, and there was a general slide into silence in communal spaces as well. During spring and summer the talk in the large public saunas was invariably upbeat and positive, but with the shortening of the days came a morose tone and a drift in subject matter away from politics, theatre and sport to discussion of how the leaves were changing colour in the city of Rovaniemi, or how the old-timers thought it would be a long winter. Much later it occurred to me that my own descent into melancholia and introspection could well have been a mild version of SAD.

Taking a sauna became a regular part of my week, and I enjoyed the conversation and companionship of total strangers; we were all equal in the heat. I grew to love it so much that I continued the ritual back home, building a sauna in Hobart and later in Brisbane. A lot of nonsense has been spoken and written about saunas and sex, and saunas and weight loss, but the actual benefits are quite different and consist mainly of boosting the body's immune system and circulation. Thanks to a weekly sauna, I go year after year without a cold or dose of influenza.

The Finnish word *sisu* is probably best translated as 'bloody-minded determination'. This quality was never more in evidence than during the frozen hell that was the Winter War. On 30 November 1939 Stalin ordered 250 000 Russian troops to cross into Finland under cover of a coordinated air and artillery bombardment. So began one of the least known and yet most costly campaigns of World War II. The Russians estimated it would take less than two weeks for their well-equipped divisions to reach Helsinki, given that the Finnish forces were ill equipped and numbered fewer than a hundred thousand men.

But the battle raged for 105 days, with the Russians dying

at a rate of some 1200 a day, against Finnish casualties of 250 a day. When the armistice finally came on 13 March 1940 the Finns counted 26 000 dead and 55 000 wounded (a terrible toll for a country of only four million people) and the Russians 127 000 dead and 264 900 wounded.

At the other end of the scale, this national characteristic of *sisu* manifests as a positive determination to get things done. Single-minded determination has its downside too, of course, and the most common example used to explain this quality to foreigners is door-opening. Your typical Finn, it is claimed, who starts to pull open a door will continue to pull even when it is pointed out that the sign says 'push'. A good trait to pick up? Well, maybe; I found that *sisu* is the best way of getting a novel written. The big difference between those who want to write a book and those who do so is *sisu*: the bloody-minded determination to get it done.

After leaving Finland I made my way back to Tasmania and settled in Hobart, where I returned to theatre work. I merged the remnants of the Illusion Circus Theatre Company with those of a colleague's to form the de facto state theatre company, Zootango. The company began its life with a production of *Hot Dogs*, which I had written in Finland. But my return to theatre was brief, and after several productions I was offered a position with the ABC.

Having worked for the ABC in Sydney, I thought I understood the culture, but I was dreadfully wrong. Metropolitan Hobart radio was nothing like Double Jay. It was staid, polite, and not at all about pushing boundaries or taking risks. I signalled my intentions pretty clearly by naming my afternoon music program *Afternoon Off*, and by adopting a business card that was as far from the standard ABC format as possible. It was pale green and had a cartoon of me in a spa bath.

I played predominantly world music on the show, which garnered a respectable following until someone higher up the chain of command decided that from now on all programs would feature music from a single playlist. It concerned me that so little trust was put in presenters: if they weren't up to programming and presenting a good show, why hire them? I needed something more challenging, and when an opportunity arose to move to Radio National I grabbed it with both hands.

In my new job I was the presenter of an adult-education program. As there is virtually no area of inquiry that can not legitimately sit under the label of adult education, the role was a natural fit for someone with my eclectic tastes. The program was called *Connexions* and for a while it had a reasonable budget, allowing my producers and me to travel and broadcast from around the nation. Ironically it was on the very day that the program was awarded the accolade of Adult Educator of the Year (which was also the day I was reunited with my daughter Cathryn after our long separation) that government cuts to the ABC caused the closure of the entire Radio National branch in Hobart.

The axing of *Connexions* came as a real blow to our broadcast team, and for a few days I considered returning to writing fulltime. Then Norman Swan, who was running Radio National at the time, threw down a challenge for me to come up with an idea for a new program. One of the strengths of *Connexions* had been its once-a-week talkback segment and this prompted me to consider a show devoted solely to talkback, but one done in a serious-minded way. I discussed the idea with a friend, who advised me to tread warily. In his opinion, Radio National considered itself a little too highbrow for talkback.

That response was like a red rag to a bull, and I immediately emailed Norman and suggested a program that would run as 'an antidote to John Laws'. I proposed that it have a philosophical base underpinned by social-justice and human-rights principles.

I had been prepared to argue the case for this on the basis of the human-rights protocols that Australia was signatory to. If this was national policy, I would maintain, then as the national broadcaster we had every right to espouse it. To my delight I had no need to debate the point: Norman supported me to the hilt.

There was some discussion as to where the program should

be located. I decided against Sydney, and as there was no free office space in Melbourne, despite new ABC premises having just been completed in the South Bank complex, I was lured to Brisbane with the promise of a purpose-built studio and my own car space, the latter not being something I cared a great deal about at the time. I moved north, and in January 1992 *Australia Talks Back* was born, with an inaugural program on Australian identity. Seven years later it was joined by the monthly *Australia Talks Books*, a virtual book club of the airwaves, co-hosted by Ramona Koval.

More than a decade on, both programs have a wide listener base and have earned the respect of both sides of mainstream politics. The role of talkback host has been an immense pleasure for me. My daily contact with thousands of people from diverse backgrounds, as well as the constant stimulation of national and international events and ideas, has few parallels in any media. Working with a dedicated team of professionals for these years has been integral to the program's success, as well as a great privilege. (But I'm still waiting for the new studio and car space.)

It's interesting to speculate, in light of the drift to conservatism in Australia in recent years, whether a program like *Australia Talks Back* would be given the go-ahead at the ABC today. How far we have moved in just ten years.

Part Two

Chapter 9

In early 1995 I got a phone call out of the blue from Mary Jane. We hadn't spoken in decades. She was living in Akaroa, near Mary, and was calling to say that our mother was ill.

Over the previous few years Mary and I had been in regular contact by mail, but I'd only visited her once in her retirement village. That had not been an easy meeting and our relationship remained, despite the warmth of her letters, fragile at best.

Mary's letters make an extraordinary collection, given the background tension. Reading them you'd be forgiven for thinking there had never been a ripple of trouble between us. Her tone was always friendly, chatty, full of gossip about old friends of mine of whom she had heard news, or of events in the life of her own circle. Golf, gardening, the snow reports from the mountains – they all had a place in her letters.

Her writing was, even in her old age, neat, tight and precise. She signed all her letters 'Mummy', executed with a flourish of an 'M' followed by a straight and energetic line that transformed at the end into a 'y'. In my darker moments I read her signature as 'mummy' flat-lined – in the manner of life-support monitors in hospitals – but any urge I might have had to pass her letters to a graphologist for analysis would vanish when I looked at my own indecipherable script. My letters to her were always typed, my signature as messy and changeable as my moods.

I flew to Christchurch, got a bus to Akaora, and dropped my luggage at a guesthouse. The day was miserable – cold and windy. Out on the harbour a southerly was whipping up white horses. Though it had been years since I walked those streets, a local Maori flashed me a smile of recognition. I remembered him as a member of the Ngai Tahu tribe from the village at Onuku, on the outskirts of Akaroa, but preoccupied as I was with my impending meeting, his name eluded me. I waved to him and walked on.

I wandered around town for a long time, putting off the moment of going to see Mary. I found distractions everywhere, but finally, after standing outside the Gaiety Theatre for about ten minutes, I turned and headed along the foreshore towards the retirement village.

The sun broke through the clouds, and by the time I arrived

at St Patrick's Church in Rue Lavaud the day was considerably brighter. I rounded the corner into the Rue Viard and the entrance to the beautifully designed and maintained Catholic retirement home, Pompallier Village. Given the McCutcheon family's openly expressed hostility to the Catholic faith, I have never understood why Mary went into a Catholic home. It might have had something to do with the fact that Mary Jane had married a Catholic, something I heard about from friends in Christchurch. I wasn't invited to the wedding, and can remember being amazed to hear that she had married the son of a Catholic family who lived near our holiday house in Akaroa. I knew, though, that it could only have been a marriage of love – rebellion was foreign to Mary Jane's nature.

On my previous visit Mary hadn't strayed far from her room, but this time she was up and about, with my sister acting as chaperone. Over the years, Mary Jane and her husband had done a wonderful job of looking after Mary, with the advantage of living only a short walk away, and now my sister was determined that I would not upset the applecart.

The last letter I'd had from Mary was in the same vein as all the others – friendly and chatty and signed, 'God bless, lots of love, Mummy'. Yet face to face there was the old feeling of distance. We wandered through St Patrick's and then went to Mary Jane's house a few doors up for a cup of tea.

Mary was frail now. Always a small woman, she reminded me of a sparrow – sharp-eyed, sharp-tongued and with a cast-iron will. 'Tough as nails' was how one family friend described her to me on her death. I heard how, when she and Mac were building the holiday house at Arthurs Pass after the war, she'd get up in the roof to nail rafters in place. It was so cold that the hammer once froze to the floor after she dropped it. When she climbed down to retrieve it she had to prise it off. She did so, and returned to her task. She was tougher then me.

After tea, I took Mary back to Pompallier Village and she suddenly said to me, 'I had to tell him he was from over there.'

Why had I been cast into the third person? Maybe that felt safer for her. In any case, I understood what she meant. She was referring to the story that I was from war-torn Europe, although this wasn't something she'd ever told me herself.

'Why?' I asked, going along with her. 'Why did you need to do that?'

'Because otherwise he would have dug around and found out the dreadful truth.'

This time I had no idea what she was referring to. I said goodbye to Mary and went back to Mary Jane's house. Where there was a bombshell awaiting me.

Mary Jane said she had something for me, and produced an envelope. I opened it and took out a large legal document. On the outside was typed:

IN THE MATTER of an application by Hugh Maitland McCutcheon of 5 Roa Road, Christchurch, Dentist and Eva Mary McCutcheon his wife to adopt Brian David Parry.

I don't remember much after that. For the first time in years I was coming down with influenza; my head was aching and I wasn't seeing or thinking straight. I think I asked Mary Jane how long she'd known about the adoption papers. Over the years, she'd been the one on the spot; she'd given Mary a hand moving, packing and unpacking. Yet she had somehow never seen the document.

I wandered down to the main beach and walked. It was getting dark and the wind had sprung up again, bringing light rain. I don't know how long I walked for, but at some point a hand grabbed my arm and guided me into the bar of the Grand Hotel. It was my friend from the Ngai Tahu tribe.

He bought me a double Scotch and coaxed the story out of me.

'Why,' I asked him, 'did I bother to come back?'

'People always come back.'

'Why?'

'*Aroha ki te iwi.*'

Love of the people. 'But they aren't even my *iwi*.'

'We always thought you were different,' he said, and added playfully, 'for a *pakeha*.'

For the next hour we drank and talked. I watched him

play snooker with other Maori men who drifted in. I still couldn't remember his name, but I will always be grateful for his kindness and warmth on the coldest night I have ever spent in Akaroa.

Eventually I wandered back to the guesthouse and fell into bed. My mind was spinning, not just from alcohol but from shock. I read and reread the adoption papers, trying to understand what was written there. But nothing made sense. I took out a notebook and attempted to write down what I was feeling. When I woke up next morning the page was blank. But I'd been dreaming a dream I'd had half my life, although not for ten years or more. I was dreaming about wolves.

I don't know where the wolves came from. Maybe all boys dream of wolves. There were no wolves in the New Zealand Alps, but perhaps there should have been.

The dream invariably begins with a storm and the rattling of shutters, then a knock at a cottage door. As I open it a man stumbles in, wild-eyed, the blood from a cut on his face frozen to his chin. All he says is, 'Wolves . . .' and I know the rest.

Somewhere out there is his wife and child. They are encircled by wolves – starving wolves with cubs to feed. Old wolves with the long winter threatening and young wolves needing to prove themselves.

I wrap the man in a blanket and put a mug of hot, rum-laced tea in his hand. He watches in silence as I take the rifle from the bracket on the wall. I check the bolt, load the magazine, and glance across as he huddles by the fire, eyes lost in flames. I turn and open the door.

The wind is tearing the night apart, yet above it I can hear the howling of the wolves. Behind me the door blows shut and I head off into the forest. In some of these dreams I am on skis, in others snowshoes, but there is always the sound of snow scrunching and cracking as it compacts beneath my weight.

The woman and child are still alive when I find them, the woman clad in tattered garments, the child, waif-like with starving eyes, clinging to her, tense and mute. They are in the ruins of a rough camp, the fire almost out, the last embers resembling the eyes of the wolves who are circling ever closer.

My first shot frightens all but the leader. Tonight he is large and white with an enormous scar down his left hind flank. He is a veteran of many winters and though he knows me and my gun, he stands defiantly on a slight rise. As I reach the woman and child, the fire dies. For a moment they cling to me, she with her head against my chest, the child silently pressed against my legs. I scoop the child up and the three of us walk towards the wolf.

The animal and I lock eyes and at the last moment he scowls and limps away. When we reach the cottage the woman takes the child from me and runs to the door. The man greets them and the last glimpse I have is through lace-curtained windows: the child, mother and father happy in their home.

I turn and trudge off into the night, looking for a new cottage, a place to call home, until another night when again a man will come and whisper, 'Wolves...'

Dreams of wolves inevitably bring to mind Freud and his famous patient Sergius Pankejeff, the Wolf Man. Pankejeff dreamed of white wolves staring at him from the bare limbs of a tree outside his window, from which he and Freud deduced latent homosexual tendencies. But dreams can be interpreted in different ways. In both Pankejeff's dream and my own it is winter, but after that the symbolism diverges. My wolves are about threat and loss of family, about children and, ultimately, the womb – the cottage.

I got out of bed and looked again at the piece of paper that held the answer I'd been looking for all my life, but which had now plunged me into the deepest confusion and an overwhelming sadness. I lay back down on the bed and howled like a wounded wolf.

Later that morning I pored over the adoption document, looking for anything that would give me a clue as to what had taken place so many years before. I needed a focus for the anger welling up in me but found little to help in the document. There were some dates and a couple of names – Colin F Hart and Frank Reid. Even though I had no idea who these men were, my fury was directed at them. On Thursday 5 May 1949 Frank Reid lodged an application for adoption with the Magistrate's Court in Christchurch, and a little over a month later, on Wednesday 8 June 1949, he signed away my life.

I couldn't help wondering how Frank had started the day. I supposed it was totally unremarkable for him. Perhaps he showered, dressed, and sat down to a hearty breakfast of bacon and eggs followed by tea and toast. And what was I doing that morning? I would have been two years, three months and nineteen days old.

After breakfast Frank headed into the city, and some time in the next few hours he added his beautifully executed signature to a document drawn up under Part III of the *Infants Act, 1908 and its Amendments*. The adoption of Brian David Parry, born 17 February 1947, was signed, sealed and delivered. In Frank's eloquent words:

AND WHEREAS all the conditions and requirements of the said Act and the rules thereunder relating to the adoption of children have been duly complied with and fulfilled, and I am satisfied of the several matters of which by the said Act I am required to be satisfied.

NOW THEREFORE, I FRANK FELIX REID, Stipendiary Magistrate, DO HEREBY ORDER AND ADJUDGE that the said male child named Brian David Parry may be and hereby is adopted by the said HUGH MAITLAND McCUTCHEON and EVA MARY McCUTCHEON and each of them under

Section 17 of the said Act as from the date hereof and shall thenceforth bear the name of ROBERT HAMISH McCUTCHEON.

From that moment on, Brian David Parry officially ceased to exist.

Now, it may be that I'm right off the mark here, but I would have thought that if someone had come into the room around that time and said, 'Hey, Brian, would you like an ice cream?' I would, at almost two and a half years of age, have responded. And that if someone had asked 'Robert' if he'd like one, I would have been looking around to see where the interloper was hiding. Most kids that age know their own name. Had I been a year younger, the new name might have stuck, but as it was, for all of Frank's earnest *now therefores*, for all his *ordering and adjudging*, the name never stuck and I was never known as Robert or Hamish.

Perhaps in my first few years in the McCutcheon household I did do my best to 'remember who I was', as I was constantly being admonished, but somewhere along the line my mind must have rebelled, and in some sort of compromise I became known as Sandy. Yet inside, Brian David Parry was fighting for survival, and in 1995 he surfaced. He was forty-eight years old. It seemed to me we had a lot of catching up to do and I determined then and there that I was going to find out everything I could.

Somehow I got back to Christchurch, and began hunting out an adoption-information service. But I was in no state to deal with the bureaucratic hurdles that immediately presented themselves. I stood in a government office, read some brochures and, unable to control my emotions, walked out. Tears were streaming down my face and yet I had no idea what I was crying for. Standing in the middle of Cathedral Square, I couldn't stop thinking about the nature of the 'dreadful truth' that Mary had spoken of. I decided on one more attempt to contact the Adoption Information Services Unit, this time by phone.

My hands were shaking as I dialled and I was not confident of being able to speak coherently. I hung up and walked around the square again. It's only a bloody phone call, I castigated myself, and strode back to the phone. This time my nerve held and I spoke to a man who listened sympathetically and suggested I put what I knew in writing. He would look into it for me, he said.

Around me Christchurch was in a late-afternoon bustle. Everybody had places to go, people to see; they all had real homes. I felt myself descend into a familiar black space. For most of my life I had been searching for my roots — in the wrong place. A wild goose chase spanning more than three decades. I had looked everywhere from Austria to Yugoslavia. I had sat in train stations and airports, bus terminals and cafés, listening to languages, clinging to the belief that, if nothing else, I would recognise my native tongue. I'd been convinced that deep inside me something would be triggered – a deeply buried memory would stir and I would be able to claim a homeland. Then, just when I had come to terms with the fact that I would never discover my real parents or my nationality, here it was, served up on a plate for me. New Zealand. Bloody New Zealand, the one place I had felt I could confidently strike off my list. Aotearoa. The Land of the Long White Cloud. And more than that, Christchurch. Now it was no longer simply the place I had grown up in, but truly my hometown. Yet now that I had this information I felt alienated, almost repulsed.

Hours ahead of time I caught a taxi to the airport, and sat as far away from everyone as I could to wait for my plane back to Brisbane. The flight was dreadful. I felt as though at any minute I would burst into tears. Such a feeling is distressing at any time, but particularly so to men who like to maintain a stoic exterior. Public tears always feel shameful, the more so when there's no obvious, external evidence of harm, no visible cause of pain.

The plane was well out over the Tasman when I realised it was not I who wanted to weep but the child inside who had been locked away for so long. Now his name had been spoken for the first time in decades. Brian. It was as though a ghost had been summoned and was demanding to be heard. But there was nobody to comfort him. He was a stranger even to me.

Despite having vowed to pursue the truth about my adoption, I spent the next twelve months in denial. I immersed myself in my writing and radio work, trying to keep myself from dwelling on the issue. When feelings did surface, they were of betrayal. Where had my biological mother been all these years? Had she given me up willingly? Did she know where I was? Why hadn't she tried to contact me? Was she even still alive? And what about my father, this Mr Parry? Where? Why? What? Who? My mind went round in circles; I felt like a child trapped in a strange room in a darkness that threatened to engulf me. The door was locked and all I could hear was silence. I clamped down on my emotions, burying them under hard work and distraction.

It seems odd to me now that I didn't push forward at the time, but perhaps denial is sometimes a coping mechanism. Later I transferred this experience to the major character in my novel *In Wolf's Clothing*, who was himself adopted. I consciously used him to explore my feelings, but I remained not only sad but angry. I had been the only one searching for the truth, yet surely there were others who had known Brian Parry existed? My birth and the first two and a half years of existence hadn't been a secret, so why had nobody come looking for me?

I added a dedication to the book that summed up what I was feeling: 'For Brian David Parry who has been working undercover in Australia and New Zealand since 1949. And for all those who have attempted, unsuccessfully, to track him down.'

It wasn't until 1997 that circumstances forced me to confront the issue again: Mary's death on 26 May of that year was the catalyst for my resuming the quest. Guessing that my sister wouldn't be welcoming, I rang my old friends Guy and Marianne Hargreaves in Christchurch and arranged to stay with them. Not only was their welcome wonderful but Guy took one look at the state I was in and offered to take the following day off work and drive me to Akaroa for the funeral.

Next morning, he handed me the newspaper and pointed to the funeral notice. 'You get a mention,' he said. 'Second class.' He indicated the wording. 'You're "loved son of". Mary Jane is "dearly loved".'

'Well, that's pretty accurate. The way I've lived my life, it's a wonder I get a mention at all.'

The funeral was held in St Peter's in Rue Balguerie, and as Guy and I entered I was struck by the beauty of the natural-wood interior and the way the morning light filled the little church with a rich golden glow. It was thirty-five years since I'd been in this place where, as children, Mary Jane and I had gone to Anglican communion with Mary on the Sundays we were in Akaroa. Mac always remained at home. I have no memory of him ever crossing the threshold of a church of any denomination.

On the slopes at Arthurs Pass

The cottage at Arthurs Pass

In my theatre days, 1960s

Guy and Cathryn, 1974

With Maha and Alia at Illusion Farm, 1970s

The gompa at Illusion Farm

Joan Isobel Parry

Morris Owen Parry

Joan with Bronwen, 1940s

With Mary and Mary Jane McCutcheon, Akaroa, 1995

Joan and Norm Penter, 1948

The pistol-packing, gambling-loving Ethel Parry (second from right), Auckland, 1940s

Top and bottom: with Glyn and Bronwen at Brisbane airport, 1999

With Alia and Arwen, Canberra, 1995

With my lifelong friend Guy Hargreaves, Christchurch, 2003

Suzanna, 1999

With Maha and David Margan, my best man when Suzanna and I got married, 1999

With Dorothy at the Pukapuka cemetery, 2000

Norm Penter, 2003

With Yvonne and Nathan, Fès, 2005

The house in Fès

The service was simple but moving, with a military guard of honour and an emphasis on Mary's war service, which came as a revelation. I had known she'd served as a nursing sister but was unaware until that morning of the bravery she'd shown during the German landing on Crete. But the most memorable part of the morning was the prayer, attributed to Mary, printed on the back of the order of service:

Lord, Thou knowest better than I know myself that I am growing older and will soon be old. Keep me from getting talkative and particularly from the fatal habit that I must say something on every occasion. Release me from the craving to try and straighten out everybody's affairs. Make me thoughtful but not moody, helpful but not bossy. With my vast store of wisdom it seems a pity not to use it all, but Thou knowest, Lord, that I want a few friends at the end. Keep my mind from the recital of endless details. Give me wings to get to the point. Seal my lips on my many aches and pains. They are increasing and my love of rehearsing them is becoming sweeter as the years go by. Teach me the glorious lesson that occasionally it is possible that I might be mistaken. Keep me reasonably sweet. I do not want to be a saint – some of them are hard to live with – but a sour old man or woman is one of the works of the devil. Give me the ability to see good things in unexpected places and talents in unexpected people. And give me, Lord, the grace to tell them so. Amen.

At the time I was too agitated to fully absorb what Mary had written. Reading it again later, I was moved by how honest her prayer was but I was no less troubled that it had taken her until just before the end of her life to give me the key to the secret of my family. Mary McCutcheon was a good women, who no doubt deserved a better son than me, and reading her prayer I felt certain that if she had only told me the truth in the beginning, it might just have been possible.

Back in Christchurch I rang my contact at the Adoption Information Services Unit and told him I was now feeling up to the task of tracing my family.

'Hang on,' he said, 'I'll dig out the file. I've done a bit of work on it for you.' When he came back on the line he told me that, according to the documents, my father's name was Morris Owen Parry and my mother was Joan Isobel.

'Joan Isobel who?'

'Parry,' he said, and then guessing what I was thinking, he laughed. 'Yes, they were married.'

'So I'm not the bastard I was made out to be,' I said, feeling suddenly light-headed. Names! I had names. Brian David Parry, son of Morris and Joan. God, it sounded so ordinary.

It was a stroke of good fortune that I'd linked up with this man who understood my predicament. This case worker, who shall remain nameless, was himself adopted and his search for his own family had led him to a career assisting others. He certainly helped me. He took all my undoubtedly obsessive behaviour in his stride, gently guiding me towards the truth.

'I wouldn't be searching for your parents,' he said.

'No?' I thought about this. 'Are you telling me both my parents are dead?'

He paused. 'No, I can't say that. I can't give you that information. But what I am saying is that it might be more fruitful to look for siblings.'

For a moment it was as though he had said something in Swahili. Siblings? I knew the meaning of the word, of course, but I had certainly never considered it in relation to myself. To suddenly do so now required a shift in thinking of colossal proportions. My universe had been centred on finding my mother, or my mother tongue, to the extent that I'd had few thoughts of even a father. But siblings? He had used the plural form, hadn't he?

'Siblings?' I finally managed.

'Yes, brothers and sisters.'

'I know what it means,' I snapped. 'Are you saying there's more than one?' The idea of any at all was startling enough – more than one was verging on the incomprehensible.

'Of course I can't tell you this, but if you happened to do

a search of the court records you'd find a document showing that a few years after your adoption, Mr McCutcheon went back to the court and attempted to adopt your siblings.'

Realising he had overstepped a boundary, I didn't push. I simply thanked him.

'A pleasure,' he said. 'And there's one other thing. Your father's occupation is listed as fishmonger.'

Fishmonger. I rolled the word around my mouth. I liked the taste of it. It had an anachronistic, working-class ring to it. Cockles and mussels alive, alive-o... No, that was Irish. Parry was a Welsh name. What did I know about the Welsh or Wales? Very little. Daffodils and leeks and coalmines. Impossibly long place names. There was a red dragon on the flag. And that bright October morning in 1966 when tragedy struck the coalmine in Aberfan. All those dead children.

For the first time I had solid information to work with, and on returning to Brisbane I began to reconsider my heritage. Having been brought up in an Anglican family, sent to a Presbyterian school, then developing a strong connection with Judaism, I considered a Welsh connection a breath of fresh air. Parry – 'son of Harry', in Welsh. A Welsh fishmonger living in Christchurch.

I had a sudden flash of the little boat the *Star of Wales* tilting and riding. Of dew falling, and the hushed town breathing. Of time passing... And I renewed my delight in Dylan Thomas for entirely new reasons.

Chapter 10

Hunting Parrys was not as easy as it seemed. Type 'Parry' into an Internet search engine and in less than a second there are 1.2 million references to choose from. It was rich pickings and offered me more distractions than even my curious mind would ever need. Among those that caught my eye were Nigel Parry, a fascinating freelance journalist and chronicler of the electronic intifada in the West Bank and Gaza; Parry Sound, where 'thirty thousand islands, lakes, towns and historic rivers' awaited my arrival; and Hubert Parry, who adapted for song the immortal lines of Richard Lovelace (1618–57):

> *Stone walls do not a prison make,*
> *Nor iron bars a cage;*
> *Minds innocent and quiet take*

That for an hermitage;
If I have freedom in my love,
And in my soul am free,
Angels alone that soar above,
Enjoy such liberty.

I wondered if these lines were of any solace to Deborah Parry, the British nurse who was at that time in a Saudi prison, accused of murdering another nurse with whom she was alleged to be having a lesbian affair. It was at the point when my search led me to Greg Parry's 'bodywear for today's active male' that I decided I needed to refine my parameters.

I did an advanced search for New Zealand and was quickly down to a much more manageable 41 500 results. Most of them, it seemed, were about Craig Parry. Wow, I thought, maybe I'm related to a famous golfer. Or the writer Lorae Parry. Now, that would be cool. The Parrys even had their own lockup – the Parry Prison in Auckland.

But there wasn't a hint of Morris or Joan. They obviously hadn't murdered anyone or written a book. I refined the search time and again but came up with nothing concrete. There were simply too many Parrys. It did not escape my attention, during the course of my search, that 'parry' was also a verb, meaning to deflect or ward off. Perhaps avoidance was a family trait.

In August 1997 I wrote to my case worker and asked him

to do a further search of the records. When his reply arrived the first paragraph dashed my hopes:

> Having now done a search of our records we have been unable to find a file on your adoption or previous circumstances. If there ever was a file it has apparently been destroyed during the department's periodic purges of old records.

So I'd either never had an official record or I had been purged. With my track record, the latter seemed the best bet. The whole venture seemed pointless. But then I read on:

> The second piece of information we found was an index card dated 12 September 1955. This records the names of three Parry children including you and was apparently filled out because your adoptive parents contacted the department to enquire what happened to your brother and sister. It states '– wished to give two eldest a home if they were in orphanages'. Someone must have checked the situation because there are some more scribbled notes about where the others were and a comment 'Information obtained via Parry enquiry file'. It is this file that we went looking for and have been unable to find.

It took a moment for the implications to sink in. I read it again carefully. The thing that leapt out at me was not the confirmation that Mac McCutcheon had tried to adopt my brother and sister, but that he knew they existed. Everything I had learned about adoptions in this era stressed how tightly privacy was protected. So, I deduced, if Mac had known about them it could only have been from one of two sources. Either the McCutcheons had had personal contact with the Parrys, thereby learning of the family's disintegration, or they knew about the other children from me.

Of course these possibilities did not have to be mutually exclusive: the request to adopt could well have been prompted by a combination of both. But until I knew more about Morris and Joan's history, I could not investigate any link between the two families. The more I thought about it, however, the more I settled on the second option. If the McCutcheons had known the Parrys, then they would also have known where the other children were. It seemed more likely that their inquiry was prompted by my behaviour. Had I still been grieving for my missing siblings? Did my disruptive behaviour lead the McCutcheons to think that this was the case? Were they genuinely concerned for my brother and sister, or were they desperate for some way to help settle down a troubled eight-year-old?

My mind in a spin, I went back to the letter:

I am not allowed to give you information about your siblings without their permission and probably the simplest way forward for you is to contact your birth parents.

That pulled me up short. In our previous conversation he had hinted they were both dead. There was a second page to the letter, which I skimmed for references to my parents, and at the end:

Hopefully you will find at least one of your birth parents alive... I'm sorry we haven't been able to find anything further and I hope that you are going ahead with a search for Morris and Joan. If you get stuck, or if we can help in any way, don't hesitate to give me a call.

Dead? Alive? At least one alive? I felt totally confused. It had been much easier dealing with the belief that they were dead. If they were alive, why weren't they trying to find me? And was it safe to believe they were alive, or was I setting myself up for another letdown?

I returned to the passages I had skipped over. There, at least, I found some solid facts. Despite having said he could give me no detail, the case worker had written:

I can tell you that your oldest sibling was a girl born in 1943 and that the card notes that she was 'with Grandmother

Auckland'. The next is a male born in 1945 and the card says 'with father 58 Buckleys Rd'. This is presumably the Buckleys Rd in Christchurch. Although we can't be sure I would presume that these details date from around 1948/49 when you were adopted.

So I was the baby of the family, and I definitely had an older brother and sister. The letter went on:

It seems to me that the most likely scenario is that up until late 1948 you were with your birth family. Around that time something happened that disrupted the family. This could have been a separation, but was just as likely your birth mother becoming ill or even dying. Whatever the case it seems your father may have been left with three children to care for. In those days men were generally not seen as being able to care for children, and of course there were no Benefits available to provide financial support, so he would have had to make alternative arrangements to look after the three of you. Hence your sister being sent to live with her grandmother and you as the youngest being placed for adoption.

Although the letter raised many more questions than answers, I was grateful for the information and speculation.

I filed it away and returned to scrambling around in family trees.

I had never attempted any serious genealogical research before now, and the thought crossed my mind that maybe I should get a professional on the case. But I was enjoying the exercise and decided to press on. I turned to the McCutcheon family, with a view to finding out when they had first set foot on New Zealand soil. There were far fewer McCutcheons than Parrys in the country, and I soon discovered that they had arrived on some of the first ships. The investigation was fascinating, but ultimately all the McCutcheons proved to be false leads.

Then something else happened to distract me from my search. A couple of months after Mary's funeral, I received a letter from a Christchurch solicitor informing me that I had been cut out of her estate. The news was more of a disappointment than a shock: Mac McCutcheon had done the same thing before he died.

On Mac's death in 1972 I was advised to contest the will, and I did so not on my own behalf but that of my two children, Guy and Cathryn. My being disinherited was understandable, but that my children should be punished because of my life choices struck me as grossly unfair.

My lawyer had informed me that under New Zealand family law a male heir could not be cut out of a will for anything other than murder or treason. As this law had never been tested before a court, the Law Society offered to run my case free of charge. I agreed and promptly forgot about the whole thing. It took several years for the case to come before the Supreme Court in Wellington. This was the late seventies and I was living on Illusion Farm. An airfare was provided and before I knew it I was in court as a witness.

The court case was surreal. Every beneficiary of my father's will had employed a high-powered lawyer to represent them. I had a young Legal Aid chap whose advice to me was, 'Get a haircut and don't admit to living in a Buddhist retreat centre where you breed goats and donkeys.' The defence lawyers competed with each other to see how much damage they could do to my credibility as a witness. The fact that I was living in Tasmania was offered as damning evidence of my dislike of New Zealand. My opposition to the Vietnam War was dragged out and every single one of the lawyers asked me about 'hippie communes'. Through all of it, Mary and Mary Jane McCutcheon sat in the gallery eyeing me with thinly veiled disgust.

Then out of the blue the judge asked Mary to directly answer the question of whether or not I was adopted. For a moment I thought she was going to refuse to answer, but she looked away from me and said quietly, 'Yes.'

It was the first time in thirty years anyone in my family had told me the truth. I sat there with tears running down my cheeks. The defence lawyers had pointed out time and again what an unloving, uncaring son I was. They'd also spared no opportunity to make clear their own repulsion at how I had broken my mother's heart, not once but many times. Yet in that quietly whispered 'yes' was all the vindication I sought. No matter which way the verdict went, I had what I'd always sought. The truth. In that instant it again went through my mind how different things might have been had I known it as a child.

The judge announced that he would be making a written judgement and the hearing was over. I waited outside in the forlorn hope that, having finally admitted I was adopted, Mary would make some sort of conciliatory overture. She and Mary Jane walked off without saying a word.

Six weeks later, I received a copy of the written judgement. Much to my surprise, and that of my lawyer, not only had I won the case on behalf of my children but the judge, far from being swayed by revelations of weird Buddhist practices in Tasmania, complimented me on my openness and the strength of my beliefs and ordered that a sum of money from Mac's estate be allotted to me. To my further amazement, Mary McCutcheon was instructed to apologise to me for having withheld the fact that I was adopted.

It is to Mary's credit that she apologised without delay. The letter she wrote me fulfilled the legal requirements but went no further; it contained no further information about my adoption. Nevertheless from then on we had what I felt was a friendly correspondence, with Mary regularly sending me cuttings of interest from the Christchurch papers. We had reached a sort of truce, and neither of us ever strayed into an area that was likely to upset it. Certainly we never wrote about the court case or my adoption again.

But now, in a letter attached to her will, she cited the judgement from that case as her basis for excluding me from her own legacy. Not once in this letter did she criticise me personally, but she claimed acerbically that I had been wrongly advised by my lawyer. It was obviously a grudge she'd held for a long time, as the letter was signed fourteen years before her death. And while she had been prompt in adhering to the judge's order to apologise to me, she had ignored his order to make over my share of Mac's inheritance. Since I hadn't gone to court back then in order to line my own pockets, I'd never bothered about the money either, and my lawyer now advised me to contest Mary's will. According to him I had an extremely good prospect of winning, but I declined. It was Mary's mind I had wanted to change, not her will.

Saddened by Mary's enduring bitterness, I went back into limbo and for several weeks let my investigations slide. Then one night in November 1997 I looked up the name 'Parry' in the New Zealand phone directory and found ten in Dunedin, twenty-eight in Christchurch, thirty-two in Wellington and sixty-four in Auckland. It seemed reasonable to start with Christchurch, and so I sent to every address there a letter inquiring about Morris Owen Parry and Joan Isobel Parry. I received a number of pleasant, helpful replies, some of which raised my hopes only to dash them. I became more and more depressed with the whole thing and once more put it on hold.

It was not until the middle of 1998 that circumstances again provided impetus for my search. My second novel, *Peace Crimes*, had been published earlier that year and my publisher, HarperCollins, organised a promotional tour to New Zealand. The date was set down for October, and while the planning for it was going ahead, I came up with a plan of my own – to find my siblings. What if I were to mention my search for my family in every interview I did, radio, television and press?

I ran the idea past my New Zealand publicist, Lorraine Steele. At first she was cautious, concerned that it might take the focus off the book. She had a good point, and as a compromise I promised to raise the matter only at the end of each interview.

'Let's see how it goes,' Lorraine said.

What transpired in terms of publicity was better than either of us had hoped for. Far from being a distraction from the novel, the story of my adoption generated longer interviews and further press coverage. But responses from family members were a different matter. Whenever I mentioned my hunt for my siblings in an interview, I came out half expecting to be told there was a phone call for me, but my brothers or sisters were obviously well tucked away.

Once more I became despondent, and began to think the task was hopeless. My mind circled the possibilities. It occurred to me that if something disastrous had happened to the family, there was every chance my siblings had also been adopted out. They might not even be called Parry any more. It was also possible they had no memory of me. Or they might be dead.

On the last day of the tour I was interviewed by one of New Zealand's finest broadcasters, Kim Hill. Kim is a national institution; her program on National Radio is heard throughout the country, and when she homed in on the story of my search I remember thinking that if this didn't work, nothing would. But again there was no response, and I flew back to Australia feeling disconsolate.

The following day, I checked my emails and found that although I might not have tracked down any Parrys, I had stirred a few memories in other people. One of the most pleasurable emails was from Jill, a friend from my earliest days in Christchurch. She and I had not seen, nor probably even thought of, each other since we were kids in Roa Road, and to suddenly have her memories conveyed across the years was not only a delightful surprise but a reassuring one. Here was confirmation of memories I held with the most slender of grips. There was in me an insecurity which fed the idea that nobody remembered me, so I got immense pleasure from knowing that Jill's crystal-clear memories of childhood included me.

Hi Sandy, what a surprise, listening to Kim Hill on my way to work. The voice was naturally unfamiliar but the subject matter, which I caught part of, was very familiar. I heard the adoption part, and Kim Hill's shock when you relayed the fact the information been held back all those years. I well remember Libby Dendle's despair as a little girl, knowing that she was adopted, which meant for her that somehow she felt she didn't belong. You obviously had much more to deal with and for much longer.

I remember you teasing me as I stood waiting at the gate in the morning for the paper to arrive. Such a mimic, showing me how I jumped about making a total fool of myself. It is amazing the trivia one remembers.

I remember well your father playing the violin, Mary Jane and your mother, so alike. I don't think I knew that you were adopted, or else wasn't aware that it was an issue.

Akaroa, which has grown and changed and is not really recognisable as the little village it was, has great memories; your father in the boat towing the skiers, and you in the 'P' class, with an inordinate amount of time spent in the water – mostly me, as you were more nimble at getting yourself up on that centre board. All good fun and worth reminiscing about over a glass or two of wine.

Jill's letter was like balm on a wound. Out of nowhere had come these memories that matched mine. And the gift of things I had forgotten. But there was more to come.

Five days later, on 20 October 1998, my publicist emailed me. She started with a line or two of chitchat about the success of the book tour and then continued: 'Now, are you sitting down? I have just been called by Kim Hill's producer, who says she's been called by the niece of Morris Owen Parry. Her name is Pauline Young, she's in Auckland.'

I stopped and reread the paragraph. The hairs on the back of my neck were bristling and I felt suddenly chill. I read on and discovered that Lorraine had attempted to get in touch with Pauline Young, but she was not answering her phone. Lorraine was now leaving it to me to follow up, after very kindly offering to do anything else that might help.

Here was my first real lead. And then I plunged into confusion. I wasn't used to having relatives. What relation was Pauline to me? My father's niece – that meant she was my cousin. I wasn't equipped to fully understand that. It seems so silly now, but at the time, in my state of bewilderment, it took me several minutes to work out the relationship. Then there were the implications. My father might not be alive, but if a cousin still was then I might also have an uncle or an aunt. To anyone who has grown up with an extended family this will all seem commonplace, but sitting alone in my home in Brisbane, it felt like a miracle.

Lorraine had given me Pauline's number in Auckland, and after a couple of hours of nervous procrastination I rang and introduced myself. Her reaction was polite, even warm, but there was a cautious tone in her voice. For a few minutes we went over the basics of name, rank and serial number. All the information about my father matched and it seemed as though I had finally found a genuine family connection.

But still I heard a reticence in her voice. Pauline was holding back, and I soon discovered that her hesitation was due to concern for my siblings. She was, she said, reluctant to give anything away until she had contacted them. She promised to do so and then ring me back within the week. I thanked her and hung up with a vague feeling of dissatisfaction.

A week seemed like a very long time to wait. I might be within a phone call of finding my brother and sister and I had to wait a whole week.

I got up and paced around my living room. I went for a swim. I tried reading but couldn't settle. Suddenly it seemed terribly important that I find my family quickly. My head was full of negative thoughts. With my luck, I convinced myself, my siblings would have died recently and all this searching would amount to nothing. Or, if they were alive, they wouldn't bother responding. 'Siblings' seemed such a clinical word. I wanted names, I wanted flesh and blood. My mood became blacker and blacker and I compounded it by drinking and smoking too much (I was still a smoker back then).

The next day was no better. Nor the next, nor the one after that. By the sixth day I was imagining that my siblings had rejected out of hand the idea of meeting some long-lost brother. Why would they want the intrusion of an unknown family member at this stage of their lives? Life had no doubt taken them on very different journeys and we'd have nothing to say to each other. They were probably unbelievably busy . . .

Impatience has always been my weak point and I found I could not stand the waiting. I had to do something. I wanted to ring Pauline and ask her why it was taking so long, but was too nervous about being rejected.

Then I thought of getting someone else to ring her. I called Guy Hargreaves in Christchurch but got no reply. I knew he hated using email, so I emailed Marianne instead, outlining my dilemma and hoping she was the sort who checked her email more than once a week. The following day a reply arrived: 'Amazing to hear from Pauline Young. I'll try to ring her tomorrow and keep you up to date.'

Relieved, I sat back and waited.

In New Zealand Marianne rang Pauline and discovered

that she still hadn't contacted my brother and sister. She was, it turned out, worried about setting up false expectations. She'd only heard about my interview with Kim Hill second-hand and didn't know what was going on.

'What if I tell them I've found their brother and he turns out not to be?' she asked Marianne. 'What if it's a hoax?'

Marianne had an idea. 'Do you know what Sandy looks like?' she asked. Pauline didn't. Marianne had a couple of newspaper clippings with photos of me and she faxed one of them to Auckland. Five minutes later her phone rang.

'Oh, my God.' Pauline sounded shaken. 'That was so spooky. I watched it coming off the fax and thought I was looking at a photograph of my grandfather. There's no doubt Sandy's a Parry. I'll ring straight away.'

At home in Brisbane I was a nervous wreck, assaulting myself with every doubt I could dredge up. I felt like a bad teenager who'd done something they'd rue for ever. Mary McCutcheon had been so against my digging up the past — she must have had her reasons. Nevertheless I checked my email every few minutes and immediately regretted doing so whenever there was nothing from New Zealand. What if Pauline had rung while I was online?

I made fresh coffee and sat beside the phone, willing it to ring and terrified that it might.

By Thursday 29 October, nine days after Lorraine had first told me about Pauline, I was completely wired. I'd drunk far too much coffee and I'd lost count of the cigarettes. Waiting for Pauline to call was excruciating. If something was going to happen I wanted it to be now. Pauline obviously didn't understand this and so I was trapped in my apartment.

Outside the weather was foul, misty drizzle alternating with heavy downpours, but going out wasn't an option anyway. I rang one of my close Brisbane friends, Bob Hartley, who finally had to interrupt my nervous babbling.

'Have you got call-waiting on your phone?'

'No.'

'Then get off the bloody thing and give them a chance to ring.'

Thanks, Bob.

Normally I would have been using my spare time to write, but that was precluded by my debilitating state of anxiety. I waited for another hour and the phone finally rang. Pauline apologised profusely for the delay and then had me scrabbling for a pen and paper.

'You have a brother and sister. Glyn and Bronwen.'

My hand was trembling as I wrote down the names.

'I rang Glyn and told him what's happened,' she said. 'I told him you'd probably give him a call.'

Probably? Yes, I probably would. 'Where is he?' I asked.

'Oh, sorry. They're both in Australia. Glyn is in Sydney

and Bronwen's in Rockhampton. I've tried to ring her a couple of times, but there's no answer. Glyn said he'd give her a call.' She paused. 'Are you still there?'

'Yes. I'm just having trouble taking it all in. Bronwen lives in Queensland? Really?'

'Yes. Funny, isn't it?' Pauline gave me the phone numbers and wished me good luck.

For the next ten minutes I couldn't think straight. My head was whirling with conflicting thoughts. I guess I was in a state of shock. Or delirium. Maybe both. I recall at one point standing in front of the bathroom mirror and watching myself repeat the names Glyn and Bronwen over and over. Tasting the syllables. Attempting them with a bad Welsh accent and then descending into a fit of giggles.

Retrieving a bottle of Finlandia vodka from the freezer, I poured myself a shot and downed it. 'Think straight, you stupid bastard,' I said out loud and reached for the phone. I rang Bob again and brought him up to date. His response was typically blunt.

'So why are you talking to me? Give them a bloody ring and then call me back.'

Here I was on the brink of making contact with my family for the first time, only to find myself paralysed by fear. How hard could making a phone call be? I spent most of my working life talking to people I didn't know on the phone.

I frittered away another half-hour doing everything

I could to put off the moment. I had a shower. I shaved. I poured another drink. Then, aware I was acting like an idiot, I picked up the phone and called Glyn.

It's hard to explain what that call was like. The voice on the other end sounded much like me. Uncannily so. It was like talking to myself. Something inside me shifted, giving me the feeling that this was the most natural thing in the world. I was talking to my brother and it was as though I had always done so. Glyn certainly didn't act as if it were strange or unusual. Comfortable is probably the nearest I can come to describing it. What we talked about is a complete blank, but we ended up agreeing to meet as soon as possible.

'I'll ring Bronwen and get her to call you,' he said.

I hung up and stood looking at the phone. I had a brother. Now that I'd actually spoken to him, it finally felt real. It was so ordinary. So wonderful. Suddenly I felt whole. But there was still my sister . . .

I hesitated for about thirty seconds and then rang the Rockhampton number. Bronwen's phone was engaged. Of course, Glyn had said he'd get her to call me. So I rang Bob and filled him in.

'Sensational,' he said. 'Now hang up and let your bloody sister give you a call.'

Up in Rockhampton Bronwen had been having a pretty ordinary day. A storm was on the way, and she was heading out for the evening when Glyn rang to tell her he'd just got off the phone from talking with their brother.

'Brother?'

'Yeah. Brian.'

'We don't have a brother called Brian.'

'No,' Glyn conceded. 'He calls himself Sandy now. Get a pen and I'll give you his number.'

Still perplexed, but conscious of her husband waiting in the car, Bronwen jotted down the number and said she'd give this Brian or Sandy a ring some time. She spent the rest of the evening sitting distractedly at a services club in Rockhampton, mulling over the news. As she later told me, her mind went over and over the past, looking for answers to questions which, as soon as they surfaced, were replaced by more questions. How old had she been when we'd been separated – four or five? Where had I been in the intervening years? Most importantly, why had I changed my name to Sandy and where did the name McCutcheon come from? As far as Bronwen knew, I had remained with my mother after the family split up. Things, as she saw them, just did not add up.

'Bloody funny name for a brother,' she mumbled to herself. 'I wonder if he wears a kilt.' The name was familiar but she couldn't place it.

Then suddenly she remembered where she'd heard it before – there was a Sandy McCutcheon who was a talkshow host on Radio National. Could he possibly be her brother? Bronwen had been listening to the show on and off for years;

she'd been listening that very morning. She felt emotionally overwhelmed: elation at the thought of finding her brother after such a long separation, followed by anger and a deep sadness for all the wasted years. Then she felt ill. Surely her brother couldn't be the same person she'd been listening to on the radio all this time. Was this some sort of joke Glyn was playing? How could a brother, not seen or heard from for fifty years, suddenly turn up with a brand new name?

Once home, she resisted the urge to pick up the phone and call my number. Even if this person was her brother, she reasoned, he might not appreciate being woken in the middle of the night, and after fifty years another day wouldn't make any difference.

Before the call, after the call – she was already putting her life into different compartments. Could one phone call change a life?

In Brisbane I had no idea of the confusion I'd caused in Bronwen, I was too busy enduring my own. At midnight I went to bed, convinced she had no desire to make contact.

The following morning Bronwen waited until she was alone in the house before making the call. She didn't want any of the family around when she spoke to me. She looked at the number on the scrap of paper in her hand, for some reason reluctant to call. She put the paper down and went to make a cup of coffee. Anything to delay the moment.

When she finally dialled my number a vaguely familiar

voice on an answering machine informed her there was no one home: 'Please leave your name and number and I'll call you back.'

'It's Bronwen here,' she said and put the receiver down, confused by a voice that sounded like Glyn's. 'You silly bitch,' she said out loud, realising what she'd done. 'How the hell can he call you back when you don't leave a number?'

But I already had her number, of course, and for the next twenty-four hours Bronwen and I played phone tag. Whereas Glyn's voice was comfortably mid-Tasman, there was no mistaking Bronwen's New Zealand vowels on my answering machine. When we finally spoke to each other it was for a very long time. Neither of us has a clear recollection of that conversation, other than that it ranged over every possible subject. I hung up feeling emotionally and physically drained, but in my excitement I found myself pacing around my living room telling myself out loud, 'I have a sister.' Over and over.

The three of us arranged to meet in Brisbane on 11 November. The days beforehand were filled with media interviews, more phone calls and a flurry of excitement. Kim Hill, who had been so instrumental in bringing us together, summoned the three of us for a radio hook-up. She'd read a piece in a New Zealand newspaper about us making contact and wanted to hear first-hand how we were feeling about it. While this was fine for me as a broadcaster, it was completely foreign territory for Bronwen and Glyn, but they handled it with remarkably good grace.

Little did they know that they were soon to become seasoned professionals. The producers of ABC TV's *Australian Story* asked if they could film the actual reunion. I had doubts about the intrusion of a camera and sound crew into what ought to be a private occasion, but since our first meeting was taking place in the arrivals lounge at Brisbane airport, it was hardly going to be private. The temptation to record the moment on film finally swayed us all, and Glyn and Bronwen agreed to the filming. If they had known just how much time it was going to take they might well have had second thoughts.

'What do you look like?' Bronwen asked in one of our phone conversations.

'Like your little brother,' I quipped. 'What about you?'

Glyn, Web-savvy and resourceful, had done a search to find out what I looked like. 'I saw a photo of you on the Internet,' he told me. 'It was weird. As it downloaded I thought it was a picture of Dad.'

Not having a computer, Bronwen had gone to a bookstore and bought copies of my first two novels, hoping there'd be a dust-jacket photo. There wasn't, but she did notice the dedication in *In Wolf's Clothing*: 'For Brian David Parry who has been working undercover . . .'

Several other relatives were going to be in Brisbane on the day we were to meet, and so I stocked up the drinks cupboard and planned what to cook. Even this was fraught. What if one of them was a vegetarian? Did they like curry? Hot? Mild? Maybe a roast would be safer. In the end I decided they'd probably have similar tastes to me – perhaps a genetic thing – so I opted for a Thai green chicken curry for the first evening, and something a little more interesting for day two. After that, well, we'd no doubt go out to eat.

A woman named Carol Parry had emailed me to say that her husband Arthur was in Brisbane and that we should meet up. Arthur was my cousin, she explained. One of them, she added ominously.

As happened with Pauline, it took me a moment to establish the connection: he was the son of my father's brother. So my father had had a brother. It was all so new, and rather daunting. But I was in the mood for discoveries, so I got in the car and drove across town for my first face-to-face meeting with a blood relative. It was an extraordinary thought. I wondered if Arthur would understand how nervous I was feeling.

Arthur, understand? He was a total delight and a complete surprise – a very imposing Maori. It took every bit of self-control I possessed not to look bewildered. Over the years I had been amused at the way my New Zealand *pakeha* friends all used the Maori word *whanau* for family. I could now use it with some justification.

Arthur, who has a huge heart, welcomed me into his home as if discovering a new cousin were the most ordinary thing in the world. Within minutes of meeting him I felt a strong bond that has grown stronger over time. A butcher by trade, Arthur had come to Australia a few weeks before, looking for a change of scenery. His wife Carol was still in New Zealand, waiting for him to organise a house and a job before joining him. Arthur's knowledge of our *whanau* was encyclopaedic, and within minutes I knew that understanding my family tree was going to involve a great deal of study. In fact the word 'tree' seemed inadequate for our family. A wild and tangled forest would be a better description – some branches had been snapped off, others judiciously pruned, yet others were branching out in odd directions with renegade vines and creepers.

'Your Uncle George was my father,' Arthur told me. 'There were four brothers.'

George had married a Maori woman from Te Waipounamu, or the Greenstone Isle – the Maori name for what the *pakehas*, in a fit of wild creativity, named the South Island. As far as my limited knowledge went, that meant that Arthur's tribal lineage was Ngai Tahu – the same as my Akaroa friend who'd taken me under his wing the day I'd gone to visit Mary.

Arthur's mother, Catherine Wallace, sounded like a formidable woman. One of fourteen children, she had been raised by her grandfather, who was at one time the superintendent of the main Christchurch prison. Catherine's mother was the last Ngai Tahu tribal princess in the South Island. Now the family tree was getting interesting.

'Everyone had a good word for Morrie,' Arthur said. 'That's Morris, your father. We called him Morrie. Reg was the youngest of the brothers. Loved the horses. So did your grandmother.'

It was going to be a while before I could absorb all the detail. To say that I enjoyed my time with Arthur is an understatement – I drove home with a broad grin on my face. And Arthur was only the first of what I now understood to be a sprawling family.

More days of waiting followed. Waiting to meet my brother and sister. Intellectually I knew who they were, but emotionally it was a very different story. Confusion, elation, sadness – I was running the gamut of emotions and most of the time I felt drained and nervous. I did not sleep well. There were so many unanswered questions, and I already knew from our phone conversations that although Bronwen and Glyn could provide a lot of information, there were still going to be blanks.

Beneath it all I kept bumping into the frightened little boy who'd been abandoned. There was no doubt anger in my emotional mix as well. It had been me who'd done all the searching, or so I was convinced, and I still didn't know anything about my parents. I'd never even seen a photo of my mother and father.

'What did Dad do?' I asked Bronwen once on the phone.

'He owned a fish shop, he had a taxi at one time, he was a magician —'

'A what?'

'He did tricks. You would have loved him. He was president of the Auckland Magicians Union.'

That sent a chill right down the length my spine. I thought of what I had written years earlier, in the cottage in the forests of Finland, about my imaginary father being a magician. Morris had certainly been good at disappearing tricks, at least.

There was so much I wanted to say to Bronwen but all that came out was, 'They have a union for magicians?'

My father was a magician, I thought to myself. My father was a taxi driver. My father was a fishmonger . . .

'And Mum?' I asked Bronwen. 'What did she do?'

She was silent. 'We'll talk about it when we get together.'

I was consumed with a desire to know everything about this stranger who was my sister. The more we talked, the clearer it became how little she had remembered of me. As far as Bronwen was concerned, she'd once had a brother, although she thought his name might have been Barry, and he had remained with her mother, from whom she'd been estranged. There was too much to discuss over the phone and I was impatient to meet face to face.

The night before the reunion I slept fitfully. Either sleep evaded me or I it; suddenly it had become a realm I did not trust myself in. For the first time I had an overwhelming fear of dying in my sleep. The racing of my heart was surely the forerunner of a massive heart attack, exquisitely timed to cheat me of meeting Bronwen and Glyn. Or an aneurism was biding its time, waiting to choke off the blood supply to my brain. Twice I got up and took painkillers. Eventually I decided that if I was going to be awake I might as well enjoy it, and so at five o'clock I made myself coffee and sat watching the dawn break.

Out of nowhere came the familiar overwhelming sadness. I had been cheated. We all had. Tears poured down my face. Suddenly cold, I crawled back to bed feeling too vulnerable to face anything.

At last I acknowledged that there was no way to escape the day, and feeling ill with apprehension, I forced myself into the shower. I was unable to eat breakfast and knew that if I kept drinking coffee I'd be jittery and speedy. And I still had a radio show to do before going to the airport: at that time, *Australia Talks Back* went to air at midday. All the while my fears mounted their final assaults. What if we clashed? What if we found we had nothing in common? Maybe they'd decided not to come. Maybe . . .

Looking back on it now, my fears seem stupid, but at the time they were very real.

Somehow I managed to get through the hour on air without cracking up, but it was a close thing. I left for the airport accompanied by the film crew from *Australian Story*. The producer could see the state I was in, but no amount of kind words from her could alleviate my distress. It was, I had convinced myself, going to be a disaster. Also with me was photojournalist Suzanna Clarke, who was covering the story for *The Courier-Mail*. She and I were involved in a wonderful relationship and had been spending a lot of time together in the previous months.

Suzanna was a great source of support in the lead-up to the meeting with my brother and sister. It can't have been easy for her; there were times when I must have appeared unhinged. Anyone who can stick with you through situations like this one is pretty special, but at that moment she knew I was unreachable, so she kept herself busy checking her cameras. I was, even with people around me, totally alone.

Even entering the airport was scary. How could a mature adult be reduced to complete social incompetence? I felt like a dribbling idiot. There was too much adrenalin coursing through my veins and I knew it would all end badly. I had boarded a runaway train that would crash at any moment and there was no way to jump off. I was later told by a friend who saw me at the airport but who had no idea what was going on that I ignored his greeting and looked right through him with the eyes of a madman.

There seemed to be far more people in the arrivals lounge than usual. I stared around at the crowd, scanning faces, trying to recognise – what? I hadn't seen photographs of either of them and was unable to imagine what they might look like. Maybe instinct would help me. Some genetic marker. Bronwen would look like . . . perhaps the woman in the long black skirt with the shoulder bag? I held her gaze too long, willing her to break into a smile. She didn't. Then I saw a short woman with long red hair moving towards me. She gave no sign of recognition. She looked spooked. At the last moment she greeted someone else and I felt relieved.

Then, after what seemed an eternity, Glyn walked into view, instantly recognisable, beaming and being tugged along by another redhead. This one had short hair and she was so obviously my big sister. There was an explosion of movement and I felt arms holding me. The rest is a blur. Fifty-plus years is a long time between hugs.

Some minutes later we were about to spill out of the airport when Suzanna, ever practical, called us back. 'Can we take another shot, without the sunglasses?'

I have always hated posing for photographs; it makes me feel self-conscious and awkward. Yet at that moment, if the photographs are anything to go by, I managed to relax and smile.

All my concern in the preceding days that spending time with Glyn and Bronwen would be strained proved to be groundless. I needn't have worried. My brother and sister put me to shame with their ability to fall into step, both physically and mentally. We walked towards the car like a family. Suzanna followed, looking for another shot. We certainly looked alike, although Glyn, slightly shorter than me, had a fuller head of hair and seemed younger even though he was older. Bronwen was a full head shorter than me and a real redhead. All three of us wore glasses, but Glyn and Bronwen were stocky whereas I was wiry.

I had a sudden flash of the nature-versus-nurture debate. How had the way we'd been brought up made us different? I couldn't wait to find out.

The trip from the airport to my apartment was bizarre. We were all overhyped, overexcited. Anyone glancing at us at traffic lights would have assumed we were high as kites, a bunch of grinning idiots. One of us would start a sentence only to have it completed by the others. Bronwen later remarked that it was as if we all had an identical sense of humour – twisted. Bad puns, it seemed, were a genetic trait. I worried briefly that we were all so manic we would burn ourselves out in a matter of hours. And then what?

The film crew joined us in my apartment and began a rapid series of interviews to catch our initial reactions. The apprehension I had felt about them being involved proved unfounded. Yes, it was strange having the meeting filmed, but it also took the attention off our interactions with each other while we settled in. And if Bronwen or Glyn had any concern about the cameras and microphones, they certainly didn't show it. Both turned out to be great media performers, even though Bronwen later admitted to being nervous.

Finally the crew packed up their equipment and left.

'Bloody hell!' Bronwen said. 'They asked me stuff I hadn't thought about for years.'

'Time for a drink,' I said. 'Or do you want coffee?'

For the rest of that unforgettable afternoon we sat on the balcony and talked. Glyn was warm and relaxed, handling the situation with such grace and ease it was almost as if we'd never been apart. Bronwen was still riding a wave of excitement; stories tumbled out of her one after the other, her eyes shining. I'd had two experiences of what felt to me like real family – when my first children were born, and when I lived on Illusion Farm with Arwen and the children of that marriage – but the experience of meeting Glyn and Bronwen was different. Those earlier situations were of my own creating, whereas my brother and sister were my birth legacy. They were what was left of my birth family. This was an incomparable feeling and I was so proud of their ability to include me openly, when it could so easily have been awkward, stilted and ghastly.

In the evening people began arriving. First came Arthur, then unknown members of my family, which was expanding by the minute.

'Fred was married to Maureen,' Bronwen was explaining. 'Maureen died a few years ago. She was my stepsister. Diane is Fred's sister . . .'

I was trying to keep up. I'd already met Diane, who owned the house where Arthur was staying.

'Fred's doing some work for the Australian navy,'

Bronwen continued. 'And this,' she turned to a man who looked for all the world like a Pavarotti clone, 'is Morris.'

'Hi.' My hand was clasped strongly.

'Morris is your stepbrother.'

'Actually, I'm your half-brother.' Morris grinned. 'Not hard to remember, I'm the only good-looking one in the family.'

'Half-brother?' Now I really was confused. For a moment I wondered if he too had Maori blood. He looked more Greek. I didn't know what to say. Here I was reeling with the pleasure of having a brother and sister and suddenly there were more. The implications of having a half-brother didn't sink in at all; my mind simply refused to take on board any further information.

But that didn't stop it being delivered.

'And you haven't met Llewellyn yet.' Glyn laughed at my surprise.

'*He's* the good-looking one,' Bronwen chimed in. 'The baby of the family.'

'Another half-brother,' Arthur explained.

My head spun. Now the family was expanding by fractions. Before I could get the details, my son Alia arrived and another round of confusing introductions took place.

So this is what family is all about, I thought as I stepped into the kitchen to attend to the meal. Birthdays would be like this. Christmas, a time I had dreaded all my life, suddenly seemed a much brighter prospect.

The doorbell rang again. It was Bob, still in his ambulance uniform.

'I don't need an ambo,' Bronwen laughed.

'Bob, meet Bronwen. Bronwen, meet Bob. She's my sister,' I added, trying to make it sound as though it were the most natural thing in the world.

'No shit, Sherlock,' Bob laughed. 'The red hair would be a dead give away, right?'

I could see those two were going to get on just fine. We all would.

Finally everyone left and we were alone, Glyn, Bronwen and me. 'So,' I asked at last, 'what happened?'

There was a long pause, before Bronwen said, 'A lot of things. Some we know and others we're going to have to find out.'

And we agreed that that was exactly what we'd do.

Chapter 11

It would be untrue to say that from then on it was plain sailing. It was not. Like all siblings, we had moments when we disagreed. Because of my overwhelming desire to know about my background and be part of my real family, I was probably intimidating, at least initially, and Bronwen and Glyn did well to withstand my enthusiasm.

    I slowly became aware that, because of events following the splitting of our family, they had both to some extent isolated themselves. We had all been damaged by our childhoods. All three of us had had the same relationship patterns – a number of partners – and Bronwen and I had both lost touch with some of our children.

    Glyn and Bronwen had decided independently of each other to come to Australia, and chiefly for the same reason that most New Zealanders cross the Tasman – because the grass is greener. Bronwen also had a second reason. After a bitter dispute with welfare agencies over her children from an earlier marriage, she needed to get away, to put the devastation behind her and make a new start. As most of her friends had already left for Australia, she decided to follow, arriving in May 1978.

Since leaving home at the age of sixteen, Bronwen had had little to do with her family, and it wasn't until she'd been in Australia for a year and had made contact with her half-brother Llewellyn, who lived in Sydney, that she discovered Glyn was also living in Sydney. He had made the move a couple of years ahead of her, and they finally met up again in 1980.

Glyn, too, had lost touch with his relatives in New Zealand. Being more reclusive and reticent by nature, it must have been a shock to have a brother like me suddenly turn up, and yet he accepted me readily. It was harder for Glyn and me to establish a relationship than it was for Bronwen and me. He lived interstate, for one thing, and for his own reasons was less interested in the family history. Once I became aware of the upheavals in his and Bronwen's own childhoods, I understood why he did not want to delve into the past.

Bronwen and I, on the other hand, were both consumed by a desire to find out what lay behind our separation, and we embarked on the quest soon after meeting.

At first we flailed around in all directions, but Bronwen, with no genealogical experience, developed a flair for it and sped ahead, leaving me in her wake. Over time our individual efforts became collaborative and brought us closer together. Despite not having kept in contact with her dozens of relatives, Bronwen at least knew their names and how each was related to the other, which got us off to a good start. What we were after was a complete picture of where we came from, but neither of us had any idea how much there was to be discovered.

Our main problem was distance. Had we both been living in New Zealand, the task would have been a lot easier. Once Bronwen had the beginnings of a family tree roughed out, I decided to go to New Zealand and meet my Parry relatives. I also wanted to see my father's grave. I didn't know where my mother was buried, but I did have the location of the family plot where my father had been laid to rest.

Suzanna and I flew to Auckland in 2001. We had got married two years before, in a wonderful rural community hall outside Mullumbimby, surrounded by our dearest friends and by music and laughter. Several of my musician friends from the Woodford folk scene provided the music, and the locals had decked the hall out with beautiful displays of flowers. What added most to my pleasure, of course, was the all-encompassing sense of family. Suzanna's welcomed me as a member and greeted with equal warmth the seven members of the Parry tribe who attended – the highest number of Australian Parrys to come together on the one occasion.

In Auckland we found ourselves immediately embraced by

the wider clan. A barbecue was arranged and I was amazed at the twenty or more cousins and other relatives that were suddenly mine to claim. Standing around in a backyard eating sausages and steak sandwiches with my relatives seemed such an extraordinary thing to be doing, and I remember having to remind myself not to grin like an idiot. My cousin Pauline was, like so many of my relations, charming and genuinely pleased that I had turned up.

Yet while it was wonderful to meet them all, I found it difficult to be surrounded by people who knew more about my background than I ever could. They had all known my father, something denied to me, and though it was heartwarming to hear them speak about him in such glowing terms, they were less forthcoming about my mother. It was only later that I realised many of them had never met her either, and only knew of her through family gossip.

'Are you going to change your name back to Brian Parry?' one of my cousins asked, a thought which had already occurred to me. But on reflection it seemed a little late to be taking on another identity.

The day after the barbecue, Suzanna and I headed north with another of my cousins, Dorothy, to see my father's grave. We set out early on the main road to Warkworth. About fifty kilometres later, Dorothy turned off the highway and took the back roads until we came to a small graveyard in a town named Pukapuka.

It was a gloriously still and sunny morning, and when I finally found myself standing before my father's grave, all my promises to myself that I would handle things in a mature way crumbled. I looked at the headstone: 'Morris Owen Parry, 8 September 1920–7 September 1965'. He had died one day short of his forty-fifth birthday. I felt devastated; a disconsolate child robbed of his birthright. The sadness welling up in me for this man I'd never known was so debilitating I went numb. I couldn't talk, even to Suzanna. Amid the sorrow and anger was frustration at the fact that my search had been centred on my mother.

On the way back to Auckland we took a detour. 'Another bit of Parry history,' Dorothy said. 'The Harry Parry Kauri Park.'

'*The* Harry Parry?' I remembered a scrap of an old folk-song about 'rare Harry Parry'.

'Your great-uncle,' Dorothy said, and then added, 'the first greenie in the family.'

We pulled up outside a large and comfortable turn-of-the-century homestead. 'It used to be called the Parry Museum, but now it's the Warkworth and District Museum,' Dorothy explained. She pointed to a huge kauri tree. 'That's what all the fuss was about.'

Kauri trees (*Agathis australis*) are now rare in New Zealand, having been prized by the Maori for building large, sea-going canoes and extensively logged by early white settlers. The tree in front of me was, Dorothy told me, more than eight hundred years old and had a girth of more than seven and a half metres. She wasn't certain of the exact height, but the first limb did not appear until eleven metres up the trunk. It was impressive, but a mere teenager in kauri terms, which can grow to more than fifty metres, have a girth of up to twenty metres, and live for two thousand years. This tree would be standing long after I became mulch.

'So what did Great-uncle Harry have to do with it?' I asked.

'He and his friend, the photographer Tudor Collins, launched a campaign to save the trees and to buy all this land for the community. As you can see, the campaign was successful.' Dorothy smiled. 'He was a particularly generous man. He never married, and when he was getting on a bit he gathered the family together for a party and gave everyone their inheritance, saying it was better for them to have it then than wait until he fell off the perch. Wonderful man. Go inside and meet him.'

Hanging on the central balcony in the museum, the photograph of Great-uncle Harry came as a bit of a shock. He looked like a dead ringer of me, and it was decidedly spooky to have a near-mirror image beaming down at me. The Parry blood certainly seemed strong. I made a vow to myself to do all I could to discover where it had sprung from.

Back in Australia I began to assemble the jigsaw. At first

the scraps of information seemed as though they would slot neatly into place and I looked forward to getting it sorted out. All the early branches of the family tree pointed to *Cymru* – Wales. The earliest Parry to come to New Zealand was John Glyn Parry, my paternal great-grandfather. He was born in 1854 into a coalmining family in Flintshire, the smallest of the northern Welsh counties. John's father had insisted his children get an education that would keep them out of the pits, and by all accounts John proved a very capable student. By the age of eleven he was appointed assistant pay clerk at a colliery, at the age of sixteen a clerk, and eventually he was drawing plans of the coal seams and the underground workings.

John Parry set sail for New Zealand in 1879 and landed at Pukapuka, where he purchased land. Before setting out, he married Annie Struthers, a widow with two sons. She and the younger of her two sons followed John on a subsequent voyage, the older son, it appears, opting to stay at home. In New Zealand the family did well, managing to acquire a big mansion before John died in 1942. (Many years later their house became a rest home.)

Annie had five sons and one daughter by her second husband. Her fourth son was John Arthur Parry, my grandfather, who was born at Pukapuka on 14 December 1884 and initially known as Johnny. Johnny spent his childhood years on the family farm, working before and after school. At the age of twelve he decided he'd had enough and headed to Auckland, where he worked at a number of jobs before signing on to a passenger liner heading to the UK. He disembarked in Liverpool with wages and tips amounting to a hundred gold sovereigns. With this vast amount of money he did no work for twelve months, instead touring the country.

After a year of sightseeing, Johnny returned to New Zealand and settled in a boarding house in Auckland, where he made an impression on the landlady. Mrs Nell Richardson's boarders were mostly sailors, and when her pretty young niece Ethel stayed with her she made sure they kept a respectable distance. But Johnny Parry, a good-looking, dark, curly-headed man of the world, was an entirely different matter. He was smitten by the country girl and Nell took every opportunity to leave the two of them alone in the parlour. As a result Elizabeth Ethel Morris and John Arthur Parry were married in 1911. It was a happy marriage and over the next few years Johnny worked his way up from barman to manager of several Auckland hotels.

Researching my family history was more enjoyable than I'd imagined. I had thought the exercise would be a dry and dusty one, but the further I went, the more I came to like the people I found. Their characters took shape in my mind; these nuggetty Welsh miners with their gritty determination and Celtic charm were coming alive. Having a family tree to climb was also cathartic. The 'me' who was writing these notes was a different person from the 'me' who had spent so many years flailing around searching for identity – any identity that felt like it fitted. The pain of my childhood was ebbing away, to be replaced by a solidity and sense of worth that had previously been all bluff.

Not that the process was all straightforward. Time and again I ran into brick walls. Fortunately Bronwen, with the same determination, had assembled a mountain of dates and she also had the habit of kicking me into gear whenever I slacked off. Just as I would be faltering, an email would arrive with some new fact or date she'd uncovered. 'I found some stuff Uncle Reg wrote,' she'd say. 'I'll send it to you.'

My late Uncle Reg, it turned out, had been an amateur historian, with a flare for adding flesh to the dry bones of genealogy.

At times I had moments of bizarre good luck. My paternal grandfather's life vanished from view after his wedding, and apart from a clinical listing of the births of his children there was little to go on. Then one morning, escaping my frustration with research, I was surfing the Internet and by chance came across a story about a boat called the *Glyn Bird*. The Parry family had always adopted the single-'n' spelling of the name Glyn and so, acting purely on instinct, I looked further. And there in the pages of the *Professional Skipper* magazine I learned that the *Glyn Bird,* built in Picton in 1911, had been sold eight years later to my branch of the Parry family at Pukapuka inlet on Mahurangi Harbour. Suddenly I was back in business.

By 1919 Johnny and Ethel had three children: William John, born in 1912; George Arthur, born in 1913; and Gwladys Minnie, born in 1918. Johnny was tiring of the hotel business and looking around for a new challenge. He found it in the music industry. In the early 1920s he became sales and service manager for the La Gloria Gramophone Company, which sold beautiful oak-cased, wind-up gramophones. This was hip. This was a very long way from the coalmines of Wales. And then, on 8 September 1920, Ethel gave birth again. Another boy, Morris Owen Parry. My father.

Meanwhile the farm at Pukapuka now had its own value-adding enterprise, the Glyn Dairy Factory. But Johnny's brothers were having difficulty getting their produce to the Auckland market by road and so they turned to the sea. The *Glyn Bird* began shipping cream and butter to the city, with each of the brothers skippering her over the years. When the Auckland Harbour Board put out a tender in 1920 for rubbish disposal in the Hauraki Gulf, my Uncle Llewelyn won the contract and the *Glyn Bird* became the founding vessel of a very successful shipping venture.

In 1933 the enterprise was doing so well that Parry Bros Ltd was formed. Its vessels carried general cargo down the coast and made the return voyage loaded with sawn timber. It was at this point that my grandfather became involved in the business, as a shipping agent in Whakatane, on the North Island's beautiful, subtropical Bay of Plenty. And it wasn't only the Parry business empire that was expanding, so was the family. A fourth son, Harry Reginald, known as Reg – the family historian – had been born in 1929, followed in 1936 by their last child, Shirley.

With the coming of World War II, things inevitably changed. In 1942 the Navy commandeered the Parrys' flat-bottomed scows, they being ideally suited for a role as invasion barges. Suddenly the shipping business was no longer profitable. My grandfather, ever a resourceful individual, made ends meet by starting a second-hand furniture store in Whakatane. At this, as in everything he turned his hand to, he was a success.

After the war, business picked up again and the company went through a very profitable phase, expanding its fleet. Over time it owned many ships, including one called *Lady Eva*. The last time the *Lady Eva* worked for the Parry company was to tow the Greenpeace flagship the *Rainbow Warrior* to its final resting place off Matauri Bay in Northland, after it was bombed by French agents. Some years later I was honoured to take part in the launch of its replacement in Hobart. At the time, of course, I knew nothing of the family connection.

In 1945, at the age of sixty-one, Grandfather Parry quit his job at Whakatane and built a two-bedroom beachhouse in Auckland. By this point I'd built up an image of him as a fit, healthy and active man, only to have this dispelled by Bronwen.

'As soon as he swung his legs out of bed in the morning,

he'd reach for a cigarette,' she told me, and described how he went through the day with a cigarette always lit, no matter what he was doing. 'Then, at the end of the day, he'd sit on the edge of the bed and stub out the final smoke. And in all that time he'd have lit only the one match.'

John Arthur Parry, having reversed his names, died as Arthur John Parry in 1956 at the age of seventy-two. I so wish I could have known him.

Grandmother Ethel Parry was by all accounts one hell of a woman. In a photograph of her walking with a group of people down Auckland's Karangahape Road she could easily be taken for Al Capone's moll – with one extraordinary difference that the photo does not reveal. In the Parry family it was Ethel who packed the pistol. A .38, no less, which is still in the family's possession. Ethel had obviously come a long way from the quiet country girl who stayed at her aunt's boarding house.

A great deal of drinking was done in the close-knit Parry circle, but Ethel was one of the exceptions. Not that she was totally abstemious – a glass or two of sherry was known to pass her lips on occasion – but while she might have fallen behind the others as far as drinking went, she surpassed them in another field. Grandma Ethel was a gambler. She would even insist on sitting down to a game of Ludo before going to work in the morning, playing for threepence a piece.

Saturday night was poker night, and the Parrys and their friends would gather in the family home at Sandringham. From early in the evening until at least two in the morning the house was dedicated to the game. While the stakes don't sound all that high in today's money, a bid limit of ten shillings a point meant that a great deal could still be won or lost. There was a piano in the house, and one of the regulars was a reasonable banjo player, so during breaks in the game a sing-along would ensue. The Parrys, so I am told, were all fine singers.

While the men were heavy smokers and drinkers, my grandfather, who now went by his second name of Arthur, kept a strict eye on behaviour, and any untoward conduct was swiftly dealt with. Drinking was fine, drunkenness was not. Early on in the evening children would dart in and out from the verandah to the tiny kitchen, hunting for something to eat, but eventually they were herded away to sleep until it was time to go home. It was from Ethel, known affectionately as Ninny to the children, that Bronwen learned to play poker.

'I remember the day well,' Bronwen told me.

It was in 1958, when Ethel was sixty-seven years old and my sister fifteen.

'We'd gone to Tokaroa to visit Aunt Shirley and we sat around a table drinking tea and playing cards. We played a couple of hands for fun, but because Ninny liked to gamble and was bored with the lack of action, we soon progressed to playing for sixpence a hand.'

For a while Bronwen won and lost as her grandmother taught her the finer points of the game, but then she noticed her pile of money was shrinking fast. Aunt Shirley was also going backwards at a rate of knots. All of a sudden Ethel was playing for real.

'Ninny dealt me a hand. I kept the ten and Jack of spades and discarded the rest. I wasn't certain I had done the right thing, but then I looked at my new cards – the Queen, King and Ace, all in spades. "What have you got?" Ninny asked when she saw me shoving a couple of sixpences into the pot. "Not sure," I replied, holding the cards close to my chest.'

At this point Shirley threw in her hand and Ethel upped the ante. Bronwen held her nerve and doubled her bet. And so it went until almost all the money was in the centre of the table. 'I'll see you,' Ethel told Bronwen, and threw her last coins on the pile.

'I laid my cards on the table,' Bronwen recalls. 'Ninny glanced at them and pushed the money towards me. All she said was, "You learn fast." That was the last time I played poker with her, because I knew there was no way I would ever win again.'

It seems, however, that Ethel taught her granddaughter well. When Bronwen was thinking of buying a computer, she sought my advice. Realising they cost more than she had, she took herself off to the Brisbane casino and the next day reported she had enough for a computer and a printer, with a modem thrown in.

When things became too dull for Grandma Ethel in Sandringham she would head downtown and pit herself against the really serious gamblers in the Chinese community. Many lesser gamblers had taken on the Chinese and been spat out the other side, but Ethel, armed with her .38 pistol, was afraid of no one. She must have had as much luck as she had skill, for legend has it that she won often and won big. There are several accounts of her arriving home in a taxi with sums of more than three thousand pounds and then refusing to go to bed all night in case she was robbed.

When it came to money, Ethel trusted nobody. Whereas Arthur, who shared her distrust of banks, buried money in a tin in the backyard, Ethel hid it around the house. She had a hundred-pound note pinned to the inside of a curtain in the bedroom for emergencies, and famously always had another hundred pinned inside her bra.

My grandfather's habit of burying his money had unfortunate consequences. One day, according to my cousin Arthur, my grandfather dug up his money to discover that the notes had all gone mouldy. My cousin remembers walking into the laundry to find Ethel in tears as she washed and ironed them.

Chapter 12

'Our mother's side of the family is devoid of anything worth writing about,' Bronwen informed me. 'There are no anecdotes; mostly it's just a lot of dates and names on certificates.'

Just a lot of dates and names on certificates. It almost made me cry. If only she knew how important names and dates had been for me. They were a starting point for reconstructing a life. But maybe Bronwen was right. The Franklins, my mother's family, weren't nearly as colourful as the Parrys. There weren't as many wonderful yarns about them.

Just at a point where I was feeling bogged down in the search, I came across an email I'd received early on from one of my Parry cousins who, playing amateur detective on my behalf, had traced a woman who was supposedly my birth mother's sister. In a fit of vagueness I'd filed the email without following up on it. Had I done so I might have found the answers to a lot of my questions a good deal earlier. I counted myself lucky that at least I hadn't deleted it.

Lorna Franklin, it appeared, was alive and well; she had married and was now known as Lorna Jermyn. When I mentioned her to Bronwen she told me she remembered her from early childhood, although she'd had no subsequent contact with her.

'Surely she'd know the story of what happened between our parents?' I said.

Bronwen promptly decided to go to New Zealand and meet up with her. She was warmly welcomed by Lorna, although our aunt knew little of the family history. But she did have one surprising piece of information. Lorna was, it transpired, not our mother's sister but her half-sister.

The constraints of work and writing kept me from meeting Lorna myself for some ten months. By that stage – it was then 2003 – Bronwen and I had pieced together much more of the puzzle and I was in a better position to know which questions to ask.

One of the traps in doing this kind of research, I learned, is the temptation to get sidetracked. My discovery that my great-grandparents on the Franklin side had sailed out of London in 1874 on a ship called the *Schichallion* is a case in point. My imagination was immediately captured by the sound of the name and I was off delving into its roots. On examination it proved to be the perfect vessel to have borne my ancestors over the oceans. The *Schichallion* was named for a faerie hill, a dark and brooding mountain at the eastern end of Rannoch Moor in Scotland. With the remains of a holy well on its lower slopes, and reputedly haunted by a phantom black dog, it was acknowledged in Celtic myth as the home of 'otherworld' beings, and has been a place of offerings to the dead since pre-Christian times. Some name for a boat!

My mother's grandfather, William Jennings, was a labourer from Oxfordshire, his wife was called Martha, and they migrated with their six-month-old daughter, Agnes. They settled in the North Island town of Hawkes Bay, and three years later had another child, Annie. In 1894 Annie, by now an attractive, plump-cheeked seventeen-year-old, fell in love with the extremely handsome Henry Franklin and found herself with child, as they used to say. They were married the following January and their first son, Lovel, was born six months later. Another year on a second son, Leo, was born, followed in time by Bert and Bessie.

Then tragically, when Lovel was only ten, Annie died, leaving Henry to raise four young children. One year later he joined the Salvation Army, and in 1908 Sergeant Major Henry Franklin remarried. Some time after the wedding, he and his new wife, Isabella Young, moved to Wellington. It was there that my mother, Joan Isobel Franklin, was born.

Joan's birth certificate gives her date of birth as 23 September 1923, but the certificate's serial number is 1927/988/2893, the first four numbers of which signify the year. What was going on? Nineteen twenty-three is not 1927. Maybe it was a mistake – a clerk had simply put the wrong year on the certificate. But what was the likelihood of that? Four years is a pretty major typing error.

There was more. Isabella was fifty-three in 1923 and although she'd been married to Henry for over fifteen years she had failed to conceive before now. She appeared an unlikely candidate for late motherhood: a strangely worded Salvation Army doctor's certificate describes her as 'generally quite healthy: well formed as to the body and head'. The same doctor also states that she was 'very short in the legs'. Just how short? Four foot, five inches. I did the conversion: 1.34 metres.

I dug out the tape measure and drew a line on the wall in the kitchen. It was very short. The height used by several dwarfism organisations as a benchmark is four foot, ten inches. That was a limbo stick that Grandmother Isabella slipped under with considerable ease.

Was it possible Isabella wasn't Joan's mother? If she wasn't, then who was? And was Henry the father? Had my mother, too, been adopted, at the age of four?

It was around this stage of the search that I went to meet Joan's half-sister. Aunt Lorna is blessed with a sparkling personality and a great sense of humour and I warmed to her within minutes of our meeting. She and her husband sat me down to a great meal and a glass of wine, after which she was happy for me to grill her about the past. Lorna was very open about her family and was intrigued with where Bronwen's and my research had taken us. When we got round to discussing her father – my grandfather, Henry Franklin – Lorna told much the same story I'd been over with Bronwen. It all sounded straightforward until we came to Grandmother Isabella's death. She had died at the age of sixty-seven.

'After Isabella died, Henry married again,' Lorna explained.

He certainly did, and with some haste. Isabella died in 1937, and nine months later Henry, aged sixty-three, married Jamesina Ross, a 42-year-old woman from Belfast. Now I knew where Lorna got those Irish eyes from. She was their only child, my mother's half-sister.

According to the official records, Henry was married three times and had two daughters and three sons. We ticked them off: Lovel, Leo, Bert and Bessie by his first wife, and Lorna by his third. But where was my mother? There was absolutely no mention of Joan. She had been expunged from the records. Or maybe she had never been included.

I felt a shudder go down my spine. This was uncannily similar to what I had experienced. Brian David Parry had ceased to exist at the stroke of a magistrate's pen. Was my adoption a repeat of my mother's history? Had she too been officially expelled from the family?

Bronwen and I had also unearthed a Salvation Army document stating that Joan had gone to live for a period with a couple in Timaru, south of Christchurch. Although we were unable to ascertain how long she lived with them, a school record gave their official position as 'guardian'.

As Bronwen continued to investigate the family stories, it became difficult to separate fact from conjecture. Some people knew only parts of a story, others had obviously been handed down garbled versions. According to one story Bronwen heard, Henry was Joan's father but by another woman, and his son Bert had claimed paternity, thereby getting his father off the hook with Isabella. Then there was the version where Bert was in fact Joan's father, which would have made Henry Joan's adoptive father as well as her biological grandfather.

It was becoming more and more like a French farce. We had no concrete details other than what was recorded on the birth certificate. And that document was no more forthcoming than my own, the one I had been given on applying for a passport. Joan's birth certificate also omitted any names of her parents, stating only her date and place of birth.

The Franklin family photographs reveal, as do the Parrys', marked similarities between individuals. The surviving photos of Henry show a handsome individual with dark, piercing eyes under heavy brows; the set of his face is angular, intelligent and confident. As Lorna was quick to point out, you had only to look at photographs of Joan to see the Franklin bloodline.

'But the family resemblance could have come from my father, with a different mother,' Lorna said. 'Look, I'll take my glasses off and you can see it in me too.' She was right. 'I remember some cloud around your mother's birth. It came out at some stage that my father had had an affair, and Joan could have been the product of that. And let's face it, my father was a very good-looking man.'

I laughed. 'And this excuses his behaviour?'

'Of course it does! These gorgeous-looking men have got to spread their seed around.'

Her laughter died away and Lorna thought for a moment. 'My memory of it is that Joan just suddenly surfaced. She wasn't ever discussed at home. I didn't even know I had a sister, or half-sister. My father never mentioned her. I was seven or eight before I even knew she existed – that was in 1946, when she arrived in Christchurch with her husband and children. It was the first time I'd set eyes on her. It's something I'm still trying to put together in my head, you know, to compartmentalise it.'

There are some things in life the truth of which you have to accept you will never discover. The mystery of Joan's parents is one of them.

There were other areas, too, where it was difficult to reconcile the different memories that were presented. Sometimes there were minor variations on a story, at others complete contradictions. Henry Franklin's house in Christchurch was a classic case of the latter. It was there that my mother and father, brother and sister stayed when they first came back to Christchurch after the war. Bronwen's memory is of a single-storey flat at the back of a shop. In Lorna's version there's an upstairs, also occupied. Whatever the configuration, it must have been a squeeze to get everyone in.

As Lorna and I talked I discovered that the first time she had seen Bronwen and Glyn was the day on which our then intact family returned to Christchurch from the North Island town of Whakatane, where Joan and her children had lived with the Parrys while my father was overseas with the army.

'I remember going down to Lyttelton with my parents to meet you all off the ferry. We brought you back to the house behind the shop in Durham Street. Your mum was very friendly with a lady who lived upstairs. She took you to visit her quite frequently.'

'And was this where the fish shop was?'

'The fish shop was in Columbo Street, opposite Sydenham Park.'

I asked Aunt Lorna if she remembered me as a child. She told me she'd once had a hand-coloured photograph of Bronwen and her standing on a pink eiderdown, each of them holding a hand of a little baby boy. 'He must have been between six and nine months old,' she said, 'and he was starkers. We're holding him up and we're smiling.'

'The little boy is smiling too?'

'Oh yes.'

I would have given anything in the world to see this photo, but it had since been lost.

Morris Parry grew up in the family home in Gribblehurst Road, Sandringham, probably attended Edendale primary school, and later New Zealand's first intermediate school, Kowhai Intermediate, which had been established two years before he was born. Given that he had two older brothers, William and George, and an older sister Gwladys, one can imagine a pretty robust family life. And the word 'imagine' is apposite here because I have nothing other than imagination to go on.

Unlike many others in the family, my father stepped lightly on the earth, leaving no discernible trail. There are times when he appears in official records, but even those are few and far between. It was not until several years after I learnt his name that I saw a photograph of him, and since then I have often felt like a blind person running my fingers over a face, attempting to read its history from the contours.

My frustration was increased by my failure to go in search of him earlier. It would always have been too late to meet him, but there were several family members alive until quite recently who had known him well but who were dead by the time I stumbled along the path. Morris's brother Bill died in 1996 at the ripe old age of eighty-four. At that stage I had only known the name Parry for a year. My father's younger brother Reg, who had been born eight years after my father, died even more recently, in 1998. I never met him either, although his interest in the family history and the notes he made have been an immense help.

My father's stint at school appears to have been a short one. Like his brother Bill, he left early, probably around the age of thirteen or fourteen, and there are no further details until he enlisted in the army in 1939. He was then nineteen years of age. How he spent the intervening five years is a mystery.

Each little discovery I made about my family, no matter how mundane, was a cause for celebration for me. Partly because, in an oblique way, I was establishing a relationship with them beyond the grave. It was a relationship that was sadly one-sided, but my need for it amounted to an almost physical yearning, which manifested itself in peculiar ways. One example is my response to the names people use for their parents. The terms 'Mummy' and 'Daddy' belong in childhood, but to this day the more adult 'Mum' and 'Dad' feel uncomfortable to me.

Looking beneath my discomfort now, I find that it is rooted in an almost impenetrable sadness. I so much want to say those words and have them answered. Or even to say them without tears welling up. Several times in my professional career I have been in war zones and felt the inevitable fear that comes with confronting your own mortality. Yet I fear that dark well of sadness more.

When Bronwen refers to Mum or Dad, my sadness is tinged with envy. How unfair, I unfairly think, that she should have known the very people I am seeking; should have smelt their skin, been touched by their hands – and remember it. I am stranded behind the barrier of more neutral terms: Mother and Father.

Although Morris enlisted in 1939, he did not go overseas to fight until 1942. Using the official histories as a guide, I managed to deduce that he trained with the 3rd Division in the Waikato region. From a base at the Te Rapa Racecourse he would have taken part in the facetiously named 'Battle of the Kaimais' in the rugged Kaimai Ranges. The muddy conditions taught the soldiers the valuable lesson that their war was going to be one of engineering and logistics.

In November 1942 they embarked for Noumea, where they spent nine months performing garrison duties. As the months went by, the level of training increased, with forced marches and mock beach assaults, accompanied at all times by the legendary New Caledonian mosquitoes, which fortunately were not malarial. According to contemporary accounts, the New Zealanders, having no previous experience in either island or jungle warfare, were making up the training manual as they went along.

When my father eventually took part in combat it would have been as part of the invasion of the Green Island Atoll, 117 miles east of Rabaul. The islands of the atoll were being used by the Japanese as a staging post for barge traffic supplying bases on Bougainville. The action by New Zealand troops took place over the period 15–20 February 1944.

Of course I don't know what my father actually did in the war, nor how he'd spent the two years before seeing action. And how, I wondered, between the training, travelling and mosquitoes, had he found time to court my mother? Hopefully he wasn't absent without leave when he married Joan Isabella Franklin in Christchurch on 17 June 1942. Joan was nineteen and Morris twenty-two.

There must have been a reasonably short but successful honeymoon, because nine months later, while my father was still overseas, Bronwen was born. Morris must also have had some subsequent leave, because Glyn was born in May 1945. According to Bronwen, my father also found time to get wounded by the Japanese.

On returning to New Zealand he was not immediately demobbed but was sent to Auckland. From there he no doubt visited Joan and the children, who were living with his parents in Whakatane. The whole family returned to Christchurch in 1946.

It's not clear how Morris and Joan could have afforded to purchase the fish shop in Columbo Street, but it may have been that his father bankrolled the venture, since he assisted all of his offspring in some manner. Aunt Lorna remembers the shop well; she would go there after school and wait until Joan had time to walk her the rest of the way home. Listening to Lorna, it was obvious that she looked up to her older sister and sought out her company.

It was during this time that my father became close friends with a man called Norman Penter, who was to play Macbeth to my father's Duncan. According to the family, Morris genuinely liked Norm Penter and described him as a 'best mate'. Some of the family stories say that Norm became a partner in the shop, but I've been unable to verify this. What occurred next is perhaps the murkiest part of the whole tale, and the hardest to decipher.

Joan was an avid dancer and, as it happened, so was Norm Penter. It was possibly this shared interest that brought them together, although it's also possible that my mother had known Norm from her earlier days in Christchurch, when she was growing up. The exact beginning of their affair is impossible to pin down, but it must have been very soon after our family's return to Christchurch. In May 1946 Joan became pregnant again, and the storm clouds had gathered over my parents' marriage to the point where Morris was not certain that he was the father of the child.

This is the part of the story I find most confusing. Even

though there is no clear indication of which month the family arrived back in Christchurch, it still seems that there would have been little time to begin and consummate an affair. Either Joan had known Norm earlier or my father was worrying needlessly. According to Lorna, Joan fell pregnant before returning to Christchurch with Morris, which raises the possibility that she had visited her family in Christchurch some time previously and met up with Norm. Without this occurrence my father would have had no cause for concern.

Lorna recalls there being a great deal of friction between Joan and her father when she came back from the North Island. Morris and Joan's visits to her father's house were particularly unpleasant.

'Joan and Dad fell out,' Lorna told me. 'They would argue, and if I walked into the room they'd suddenly go silent, but you could feel the atmosphere. He would have frowned on her having an affair outside of marriage, and I remember that Norm Penter was on the horizon at that stage. I can remember him being round home.'

'How did you meet Norm?' I asked.

'I remember him coming to visit Morrie. Norm had flat hair and was rather sour. If he smiled he would have cracked his face. But I remember Joan and Morrie most. I only knew your mum for a short time. I was seven or eight and she was so much older. She was tall, with very dark hair and dark eyes – chestnut hair, very attractive. I remember Morrie as having a bit more hair than you. Tight and curly. A soft, gingery colour. He never got annoyed, whatever happened. Not once. There was never a bad word from him. He was a quiet sort of bloke, yet more fun than, say, Norm Penter. Norm was a grumpy bugger.'

'And what about later?'

'After the shop was sold, Joan and Morrie moved out to a farm. I stopped going to the shop then.'

I made a mental note to find out about this farm. I vaguely remembered Bronwen saying they had moved out of the city. Lorna knew little about the place other than it was pretty basic.

It was into this tense family atmosphere that I was born, on 17 February 1947. The fish shop was probably sold around then, and some time the following year my father and mother separated. Morris took charge of my brother and sister.

Initially Glyn remained with him while Bronwen went to Auckland and into the care of her grandparents, Arthur and Ethel. Bronwen was only four and a half years old but has a crystal-clear memory of the journey, right down to the clothes she was wearing and the fact that she was seasick on the ferry.

I was left with my mother, who moved in with Norm. In the new love nest the offspring of the previous mate was no doubt unwelcome, and after some unpleasant scenes I was adopted by the McCutcheon family. A sad but simple story.

Or was it that simple?

Chapter 13

When I began to delve beneath the surface the story got curiouser and curiouser. Different people had different versions and there seemed to be nobody alive who could verify anything but the statistics from government records and graveyards.

Mary McCutcheon had claimed she hid my adoption from me so that I wouldn't 'dig around and discover the dreadful truth'. Was this dreadful truth that I was unwanted because I got in the way of my mother's new love life? Was it that I came from a 'broken home', or from what they considered to be the 'wrong side of the tracks'? Was it all just a puritanical social stigma, a hangover from 1950s Christchurch mores? No, I thought, there had to be more to it than that.

Having watched the devastation visited on friends who have gone through a family break-up (and having experienced it myself), I know that the anguish endured by the Parry family between 1946 and 1950 must have been horrific. Glyn and Bronwen were too young to understand what was happening or to heed the warning signs. Uprooted by the war and shifted around the country from one island to the other, they would both have been too busy adapting to new circumstances to notice what their mother and father were going through. For Glyn and Bronwen, no less than for myself, our parents' separation heralded the start of a turbulent period from which they never fully recovered.

The exact sequence of events is confused, but the tremors began soon after the family arrived back in Christchurch in 1946. Towards the end of 1947, when I was around ten months old, things began to show a marked change for the worse. The tension between Morris and Joan got bad enough for my father to sell the fish shop and move the family out of the city. If his intention had been to give the marriage space and time to recover, the move could hardly have been worse.

Work was difficult to obtain at that time, and perhaps Morris had little choice in taking a job in a pine plantation in West Melton, twenty-three kilometres west of Christchurch. Glyn and Bronwen remember a dilapidated weatherboard with no running water or electricity.

If the house itself was a shock, worse was to follow. Within months an earthquake struck the area, extensively damaging the house and forcing the family back to Christchurch. This time they moved in with Joan's parents and half-sister Lorna, where the cramped and crowded conditions no doubt added to the pressures on their marriage. It was at this time, Lorna told me, that her father's relationship with Joan hit rock-bottom.

Somehow Morris managed to find work, possibly as a driver or conductor of trams or buses. But it was a short-lived period of relative calm, and not long afterwards the family was shattered. From that time on my father's life became increasingly difficult. After settling his affairs in Christchurch, he plunged into a gypsy existence in search of work, Glyn in tow. This proved too difficult and so Glyn joined Bronwen at his grandmother's house.

For a while Morris moved from property to property in the Waikato region, working as a sharemilker, until in July 1951, his divorce finalised, he married Irene Cudby. Although this relieved the strain of looking after the children alone, the family still had to keep on the move. Glyn and Bronwen joined them on the constant search for work. Their accommodation varied from farm cottages and rented houses to rooms with relatives and a transit camp, until finally they were allocated a state house in the Auckland suburb of Panmure. Between 1951 and 1953 they changed addresses every couple of months.

For both Glyn and Bronwen, Irene was problematic right from the start. When she met Morris she already had three children and was expecting another. To say she disliked and resented Morris's children would be an understatement, but however understandable her resentment may be, her violence towards them is not. Irene systematically beat and traumatised Glyn and Bronwen, and threatened them with worse if they so much as breathed a word of it to their father.

Morris, never a man to exact physical punishment, would have been furious had he known. Once, when Irene demanded that Glyn be punished, Morris took him into the bedroom and proceeded to whip the bed with his belt while instructing Glyn to yell out. Were the level of abuse meted out to Glyn and Bronwen taking place today, Irene would find herself in court, and probably undergoing psychological treatment.

Hearing the horrific descriptions of Glyn and Bronwen's life with Irene (which I have not gone into here in full, it being their story to tell), I naturally reflected on how fortunate I had been with the McCutcheons. It is of course impossible to say which option, had I been able to choose, would have turned out the better for me, but what I can say is that even knowing what I do now I still think I would have preferred to grow up with my birth family. Knowing who you are seems to me such a fundamental part of being a complete person. For Bronwen and Glyn the bad times eventually ended, and they emerged battered but in no doubt about who they were. Of course the choice is hypothetical, but I think I would have opted for being a whole person in a bad situation rather than feeling like only half a person for most of my life.

The consequences for all three of us would inevitably

have been different had I not been adopted, but in the end family is at the heart of identity. There have been so many 'if only's to speculate on, and although I know that nothing can be changed by pondering them, this has done little to stop my mind canvassing the possibilities. If my father had not doubted that he was my father... If my mother, knowing that he was, had told him the truth at once... So many hopeless lines of conjecture.

In December 1953 Irene gave birth to another child, my half-brother Llewellyn. The arrival of a son must have raised some complex emotions in my father. The boy had ginger hair and freckles, and was destined to develop an infectious sense of humour. Was this a replacement for the child he had lost? Whatever Morris's emotional response, the birth of Llewellyn coincided with a change of fortune for the family. In a stroke of luck my father won a taxi licence in a government lottery. Things began to look up, and by all accounts he enjoyed the job and the interaction it gave him with a wide range of people.

Between the demands of work and family Morris continued his lifelong interest in magic, and although I have been unable to find any documentary proof, Glyn too is adamant that Morris was the president of a branch of the New Zealand Magicians Union. (Bronwen thinks this was the Auckland branch.) We do know that he performed for groups of Maori children, and Bronwen recalls that he sometimes appeared at parties and other occasions.

'I saw him doing his stuff at a wedding, and at other family gatherings – when Irene wasn't around. He did do some practising at home, though not a lot. He got right into it after I moved out. He had these Chinese rings, the ones that look solid, but he could take them apart and put them together. He was very good with card tricks; in fact, he was extremely good.'

By the early 1960s my father had discovered that Irene was abusing his children and things between them cooled considerably. Although they remained married, Morris had a lover. This relationship was accepted by most in the family, and the woman, whose name has faded from everyone's memory, is remembered as having a great sense of humour. Irene, on the other hand, was on the outer with the broader Parry clan.

Morris was tiring of the taxi business by this time, and although he retained his licence he had someone else do the driving for him. His next venture was to buy a shop containing a general store and a coffee lounge in the suburb of Grey Lynn. This proved to be a successful enterprise, but his health was deteriorating and when he was diagnosed with bowel cancer he sold the shop and bought a house in Point Chevalier. For a while he returned to taxi-driving, but this too eventually became too much and he sold the licence not long before he died.

Irene Cudby died in 2001, but Bronwen managed to speak to her in 1999, at which time she gave a different version of the events surrounding our parents' fish shop. According to Irene, the shop had been in existence during the war, Norm Penter having stepped in to look after it while Morris was in the army. He also 'looked after' my mother, Irene claimed. How he did this when she was supposedly in Whakatane for the duration of the war is unclear, although it's likely she returned to Christchurch to visit her family. In Irene's version of the story, when the war ended and Morris was finally demobbed, he returned to Christchurch to find the shop sold and the money gone.

Then, when Morris found out about the affair, he took the two older children away. It was Irene's contention that my mother took me with her when she moved in with Norm because she wanted a baby and Morris believed that I was Norm's child.

As for my subsequent adoption, Irene claimed that Norm didn't want me, and that my mother knew a wealthy Christchurch couple who were desperate for a child. After my father had signed the adoption papers, she told him that I was indeed his son. Understandably, this upset my father considerably.

Irene's account is an interesting one if for no other reason than her claim that Joan 'knew a wealthy Christchurch couple'. This added credence to there being a connection between the Parrys and the McCutcheons, but I did not get a chance to ask Irene about this before her death.

My parents' divorce was finalised four months after I

was adopted out. Norm Penter and my mother were married the following year. From this distance it all looks to have happened with unseemly haste.

My father's version of the story, as remembered by Bronwen, was typical of the self-deprecatory humour which is a hallmark of the Parry family. Morris claimed that Joan loved the fish shop more than she loved him, and that when he sold it to Norm she married him in order to keep the shop. Yet later, when Bronwen visited Norm and Joan in the 1950s, they did indeed have a fish shop but it was in Wentworth Street, Ilam, rather than Columbo Street where the original had been.

It seemed the only way to get to the bottom of the story was to meet Norm Penter.

Chapter 14

In her flurry of digging around, Bronwen had discovered that we had another two half-brothers, Barry and Philip, the sons of Joan and Norm. Both men now lived in Western Australia – as far away from Christchurch as you could get and still be in Australia. Bronwen contacted them both, and while Philip was reluctant to talk about his family, Barry was much more forthcoming. He and Bronwen spoke by phone and later had email conversations, which I eventually joined.

Barry thought it possible that Joan had come back to Christchurch from time to time during the war and become pregnant to Norm Penter. Going by the strong physical resemblance between Bronwen and myself, and also my similarity to Morris, I had never doubted who my real father was. But

Barry Penter was not so convinced, and suggested we all have a DNA profile taken.

When the result came back it was a relief to have at least one part of the story put beyond doubt:

> The DNA profiling data obtained in this case indicate that Mr Barry Norman Penter and Robert Hamish McCutcheon are half siblings and that Ms Bronwen Joan Watson and Robert Hamish McCutcheon are full siblings ... in our view Barry Norman Penter is probably also a half sibling of Bronwen Joan Watson.

I would have welcomed having Barry as a full brother, but half was better than nothing.

Armed with a camera, tape recorder and a list of questions, I set out to visit Norm Penter in January 2003. Arriving in Christchurch, I was flooded with unsettling feelings. Now that I knew so much more about my background, the city seemed foreign, almost hostile.

This was the place where my life and that of my brother and sister had been irrevocably altered. It was the city in which my parents had lived, in which I had been born. As I walked the streets, I attempted to weave the associations together, but the threads were old and the resulting garment was ragged, frayed at the edges. Even the light seemed different now – unreal, as though what surrounded me were a painting faded by time, the original pigment having lost its potency. I was spooked.

I realised that I was scared of my impending meeting with Norm Penter. Having located his house on a street map, I borrowed a car and drove over, but instead of going inside I walked past the gate and convinced myself he was not at home. This piece of self-deception was easily achieved as Norm Penter's modest little house was at the end of a small lane, securely hidden behind a fence that blocked almost all view of it. I did a second stroll up and down the lane, persuaded myself that it had been a worthwhile reconnoitre, and returned to the car.

When things get emotionally tough I fall back into my usual patterns of behaviour. I divert my attention elsewhere. When it came to a choice between confronting Norm Penter and going fishing, fishing prevailed every time. It prevailed for several days in a row. I caught no fish but I succeeded in my diversionary tactics.

Fly fishing is a particularly contemplative pastime. Lake Sarah, on the road to Arthurs Pass, is a small lake set like a cerulean jewel in a clasp of alpine peaks. Standing thigh-deep in chill water for hours on end gave me the space I needed to face my fears.

There had been many occasions over the years when I'd put off following up on information that might have given me answers, such as the email from my cousin about Lorna.

I would always get round to it eventually, but my initial reaction was inevitably one of fear. Fear of what I might discover, and fear that I would once again come up against a dead end. Looking back, it's easy to castigate myself for this inaction, but I can also see that it was in part due to my inner turmoil, which stymied me, prevented me from moving forward. Norm Penter was a classic example of this fear-induced inertia.

But why should I be so afraid of this elderly man I'd not seen since I was an infant? It was obviously more than shyness. Norm Penter had been one of my father's friends and yet he had betrayed that friendship. This was the man whose affair with my mother had split our family down the middle and sent us in different directions. A man who for many years had been my mother's husband and was the father of my two half-brothers.

Another source of hesitation was the impression of Norm I'd gained from talking with Barry. On the couple of occasions that Barry visited me, he struck me as an extremely bright and talented individual, but with a dark and bitter streak that came to the fore whenever the subject of his father was raised. He and Norm had had their differences, and Barry made no secret of the fact that he thought my visiting Norm would not produce anything. He and his brother Philip appeared to want little to do with their father.

My biggest fear, I had to admit, lay at a deeper level. As a very young child I had received a nasty blow to the head that left a discernible bump at the back of my skull. Over the years people had remarked on the odd disfigurement, but it was not until the 1980s that I received a professional opinion on it. A doctor in Hobart with whom I played royal tennis asked if he could examine my skull, and after running his fingers over the bump, he opined that I had most probably suffered a cracked skull as a very young infant. Because of the way the bone had healed, the doctor thought it likely that the fracture had occurred before the age at which I was adopted. I was left with the unpleasant suspicion that it might not have been accidental. Had I been assaulted as a child? I thought of the dreams I'd had in Finland – my mother being dragged away, and me losing consciousness after a blow to the head. I was determined to question Norm Penter about it.

As I fished I rehearsed how I would approach him, how I would raise my questions about him and my mother. The more I thought about it, the more appealing another day's fishing seemed.

I managed to delay my visit to Norm Penter until my final day in Christchurch, and when I finally went I took backup. Feeling physically sick, I prevailed on Marianne Hargreaves to come with me. I had lain awake half the night going over what I would say to Norm to convince him to talk with me, and I was a little on the tired side.

'I really don't feel it would be safe to let me drive your car . . .' I did not need to go further. Marianne had only to look at me: pale, drawn, eyes ringed from lack of sleep.

'I'll drive.'

'Are you sure?'

She smiled. 'I've heard so much about this chap in the last few days I really want to see what he looks like.'

So it was that I arrived chaperoned at Norm Penter's door. There was no doubt this time that he was home. A small red car was in the drive. I felt the exhaust. It was still hot, as if it had arrived only a few minutes before. We unlatched the gate and walked to the door.

'Here, take this.' I handed Marianne the palmtop computer I used for taking notes when travelling. 'It has a small camera. Just take a couple of shots when he opens the door.'

I was convinced we wouldn't get past the front door. Back in Australia Barry had said as much. 'There's no point,' he'd told me. 'He won't see you.'

We stood in front of the door. 'You have to knock,' Marianne said.

Right. With my heart racing and the weirdest feeling that at any minute I might faint, have a heart attack, or both, I knocked and stepped back. A long way back.

Marianne was examining the palmtop. 'How do you work this thing?'

I slid the camera into the ready position. 'Just press this —'

The door opened and a man peered suspiciously through a flyscreen. 'Yes?'

'Hi,' I said. I've always been great at opening lines.

'Yes?' he repeated.

'Are you Norm Penter?' It came out a bit like something on a TV cop show. 'I know your son, Barry. I'm just visiting from Australia.'

Before I could build up a head of steam and launch into my prepared piece, Norm smiled and swung open the door. 'You'd better come in.' He turned and preceded us into the house.

'Which button do I press again?' Marianne asked.

'That one.' I pointed. 'Take some inside. I don't think he'll notice.'

The next thing I knew, we were sitting on a low couch in Norm's living room. He looked a great deal younger than I'd expected, and from the way he moved he was fit and healthy. He was on the short side, and had an open face and a pair of exceptionally bright eyes.

'My girlfriend has dementia,' he explained as he began sorting out some women's clothes. 'I've just taken some food over to her and brought her washing back to iron.'

Ironing? Food delivery? This didn't sound like the behaviour of a man I'd painted in my mind as some kind of ogre. It undercut me completely.

'Your girlfriend?' I asked him.

'We've been going out for quite a few years. Dancing,' Norm elaborated. 'She's Chinese,' he added and fixed me with a stare to see if I harboured any racist feelings. Anti-Asian feeling was on the rise in Christchurch and had reached the point where Avonhead, a suburb in which many Asians lived, was openly being referred to as Asianhead.

'Was she a good dancer?' I asked, for want of something better to say.

For a moment I thought he hadn't heard me. He fished around in a cupboard and produced a pile of old vinyl LPs. 'These,' he said. 'She loved these.'

There was a silence, and then I took a deep breath and said, 'Actually, Norm, we have met before.'

He stared at me, squinting. 'No, I don't think so.'

'I'm your former wife Joan's son,' I told him. 'Brian. Brian Parry.' I watched his face and I swear he didn't even bat an eyelid.

'That's interesting.' No hesitation. No pause. 'Of course that was a long time ago. She was a very good dancer. Really loved it. We went to the Riccarton Club every week. That's where she met the Dutch fellow. I have photographs somewhere.'

He rose and pulled a shoebox from a drawer and began to sort through it. 'Here. That's the wedding. Good cook too. Choux pastry. Very good with pastries.'

He handed me a photograph and a shiver went down my spine. Here in my hands was a photograph of my mother. Then another, and another. I felt undermined, bushwhacked. All those questions I had to ask, and now all I wanted to do was look at the pictures. I handed them to Marianne and pulled myself together.

'What happened to the shop? The fish shop?'

'I don't remember,' Norm said and held my gaze.

'You looked after it while Morris was in the army —'

'Morris wasn't in the army.'

'What?' I knew this wasn't true. Back in Australia Bronwen had a copy of my father's army number and service dates.

Norm fiddled with the photographs for a moment and then said something that floored me. 'I didn't love her, of course.'

'My mother?'

He nodded. 'Joan. Just doing the right thing, really. Someone had to rescue her.'

'Rescue her from what?'

'Family was in a dreadful mess. So I stepped in, really just to help her out. But I never loved her.'

'But you were married to her for thirty years. You had two children.'

'Just doing the right thing. She liked the drink a lot. A terrible lot. Gin, mostly. But it was the men. Too many men. Couldn't help herself. That's why I kicked her out in the end.'

'You kicked her out?'

'Well, it was the Dutch fellow. We used to dance with them at the Riccarton Club. Him and his wife. But Joan took too much of a shine to him and he left his wife. I'd had enough of her by then.'

I was dumbstruck. First I was told that my father wasn't in the army and now that my mother was a – what? A gin-drinking tart? I glanced at Marianne and saw that she was as gobsmacked as I was. There was nothing to do but press on. Now, however, I felt no need to beat around the bush. 'Norm, why did you and Joan adopt me out?'

'She didn't want you.'

Blunt as you like. Not one for cushioning a blow, this Mr Penter.

'You were Morris's kid and she'd moved on. She was with me. I think she felt you got in the way.'

I put my reaction to that aside to deal with at a later time. 'How did she know the McCutcheon family?'

'I don't remember the details. It was a long time ago.'

'Do you remember anything about me being hit, or having an injury to my head?'

'No. I don't remember that. As I said, it was a long time ago and I don't think it's worth raking over the past.'

There was silence again, and then he talked about Joan's illness and how when she had been dying he had reconciled with her and nursed her for her last few months. Contradictory sets of images were forming in my head. Here was a man who claimed to have had no feelings for the woman he'd married and fathered children with, and yet he professed to have cared for her while she died. And it wasn't as though he was a debilitated old man with memory loss or dementia. Norm

Penter had all of his faculties and then some. He struck me as being very sharp. His constant refrain of 'I don't remember' did not convince me at all, and I've always thought that it's those who advise against raking over the past who have something worth raking for.

Beside me Marianne had figured out the palmtop camera and was quietly taking shots of the old photographs. However, I wanted the originals. It was suddenly critical that I be able to hold them in my hands and spend as long as I liked deciphering everything they had to offer. Should I ask Norm if I could have them? Should I just take them?

While I was contemplating this ignoble thought, Norm said quietly, 'Oh, you can take any of the photos of Joan. I certainly don't want them.'

We chatted for a while longer and then went out the back into the sunlight so that Marianne could take a photograph of Norm with her own camera. He was more than happy to oblige. I stood beside him and smiled.

Back in the car Marianne and I sat and looked at each other. 'Do you believe what just happened?' she asked.

'No.' It was too bizarre. Norm Penter had been unflappable. He had demolished my mother in front of me without a single concession to diplomacy, or any consideration of the possibility that I might possess the odd human feeling. But he had given me photographs of my mother, and for that I was in his debt.

Later I talked with Bronwen, who was indignant at Norm's claim that our father had never been in the army. And she had another piece of information. Norm, it seemed, had been less than straight with me about our mother's death. According to Barry and Philip, Norm had wanted nothing to do with Joan when she was dying, from a melanoma. It had been Philip who looked after her and sat with her on the day she died.

It is a sad testimony to how shattered our family became after my mother and father separated that at the time Bronwen and I were reunited, not even she knew that our mother was dead. We first learned of it in an email in December 1998 from our cousin Pauline, who had known about Joan's death since the day it happened ten years earlier.

My mother's ashes, I discovered, were interred under a beautiful white tulip tree in a memorial garden at the Harewood Crematorium, just a short distance from where Mary McCutcheon used to play golf.

Chapter 15

There is an Afrikaans proverb that says, *Moenie die bobbejaan agter the berg gaan haal nie.* Literally, Do not go and fetch the baboon from behind the mountain. Figuratively, Don't go looking for something which is only going to cause trouble. Over the years, a lot of people have put variations on that theme to me. Why, they ask, do I want to go poking around in the past? What good will it do to dig up things that are so painful? Why not just get on with my life?

In truth there were times when I came close to thinking they were right, but now, having come so far, I have no regrets. Yes, I have roused a few ghosts from their slumber, and have had to deal with those who think the baboon should have been left as far behind the mountain as possible, but in general my endeavour has been met with sympathy and helpful collaboration by the contemporary members of my family. And the effect on me has been profound. Sometimes it's only the absence of something that makes you aware it existed in the first place. This was true of my inner agitation.

After meeting Bronwen and Glyn, something shifted deep within me and a gradual process of settling began. It was only then that I became aware of just how driven and frenetic my mental state had been. I had always excused this as being an innate part of the high-energy individual I was. My metabolism was naturally speedy, or so I convinced myself. But slowly it became clear that this was not the case. A centre of tranquillity and contentment grew within me, developing into an all-pervading serenity.

For a while, this paradoxically induced a mild panic in me. What would happen to my writing if I became content? Would I be happy to just settle back and grow old and plump? This fear proved groundless and I discovered that an inner peace does not necessarily lead to an inactive life. On the contrary, my energy levels went up because I was no longer drained by the effort of suppressing my disquiet. The dis-ease that had become so much a part of my being evaporated and I felt centred and clear. The energy I had always devoted to my work was intact. It was a great relief.

But the discovery of my birth family will always be tinged with an indelible sadness that I never knew my mother and father. My mother seems to have been a woman who lived her life to the full, and though some of her choices might have been foolish, they were her choices. Did she make the decision to give me up for adoption with her own welfare in mind? Or because she was under intense pressure from Norm? They were beginning a new life together and no doubt he had expectations of having his own children with her. Here was a cruel and egocentric man and a woman eager to please him. She had initially clung onto her youngest child, even causing his real father to doubt his paternity in order to keep him. Then a few months later she gave him up.

It seems erratic behaviour. In the animal world there are species in which new mates kill the offspring of previous males, and we see degrees of this in the clashes that often arise with step-parenting. Was this what Joan went through? Did Norm make her promise never to mention my name again? Did she have to throw out everything that reminded her of me? If so, I can't begin to imagine the pain she must have felt.

Then, too, having made the decision to give me up, she found me a family in which my material prospects were far greater than anything she could offer. Had she ever considered sending me back to live with my father, with my brother and sister? Did Morris perhaps continue to believe that I was not his child, and therefore want nothing to do with me?

My heart breaks when I think what it must have been like to have a person like my father in your life. The man who emerged from the research comes across as a real battler. He was presented with a shit of a life in many ways, partly due to the times – the war, the depressed economic conditions, the morality of the age. I often imagine him living twenty or so years later, watching the world and technology unfold in ways more magical than anything he could perform on stage. I imagine I am a boy again, being told a story at bedtime by my father. Watching him shave. Simple things. And I imagine him seeing what I have become. Would he have been proud of my driving desire to be a writer, a storyteller? Would he have understood?

In 2004 I was listening to Radio National's excellent Indigenous program, *Awaye*, and heard the Canadian storyteller Thomas King talk about his lifelong search for his father. He used to fantasise about walking into a bar and finding his father sitting there. Knowing the old man didn't recognise him, Thomas would sit next to him, share a beer and some chitchat. He'd stay talking until the old man's eyes lit up and recognition dawned. At that point the son would get up and walk away, denying his father the chance to reconcile.

For a long time my anger might have taken me down that same path. But only so far: I could never, even in a fantasy, have walked away. My longing was too great. Yet we tell ourselves stories that protect our anger more than they expose our love, or even acknowledge our loss.

Nothing can describe the pleasure I get from knowing my

brothers, half-brothers and sister. Hopefully the universe will crack open a little more and allow the space and time for me to get to know my brothers in the way I do Bronwen. The issues for them are in every way as complex as those I have had to work through, and we probably have to deal with sibling rivalry at an age when most people have left it far behind, but I am certain we can do that.

That it could all so easily have been different is tantalising. There's the McCutcheons' attempt to adopt Bronwen and Glyn in 1955. Why had they done this? How would our lives have turned out if they'd succeeded? Bronwen once told me she would have given anything to have been adopted as well, such was the pain in her life following the family's break-up.

That the McCutcheons chose not to be open about my adoption must be seen in the context of the times. Christchurch society was then extremely conservative and held strongly to beliefs that now seem not only outdated but harmful, and to judge Mac and Mary by today's standards would be less than fair. They took on a child who, because of his age, was always going to be problematic. I have no doubt that had I been an infant, things would have been different. I would not have had the subconscious knowledge that I'd been abandoned, and might therefore have settled into the family more easily.

My sister Mary Jane's attitude to her adoption is so different from my own that I've always thought it must be due to something more complex than just personality. While I've never known for sure the details surrounding her adoption, my instinct is that she was adopted at birth or at least shortly thereafter. Her acceptance of her situation strikes me as having much to do with this, and with the fact that the McCutcheons were more forthcoming with the details of her birth family. Perhaps, for her, just knowing where to look obviated the need to do so.

There's one more question that I haven't been able to answer and that is why the McCutcheons adopted me in the first place. Adopting a child because they were unable to have their own is understandable, but why adopt a child who was more than two years old? How did they even know I existed and was available for adoption? Bronwen and I have looked at this from every possible angle and are still unable to draw a conclusion. For a while it seemed that the McCutcheons might have met Joan at Akaroa, but we've been unable to rule this in or out. There's no direct evidence; Norm did have a small weekend shack but it was not in Akaroa.

Whether Norm or Joan were patients of Mac McCutcheon is also impossible to ascertain, but even if they were, the idea that Mac would have casually mentioned to a patient that he was looking to adopt is ludicrous. It's conceivable that Mary McCutcheon could have bought fish from the fish shop, although she's much more likely to have shopped in Riccarton or Fendalton. The family story that 'Joan knew this rich couple' is all we have to go on. Whether the McCutcheons looked elsewhere or were on a waiting list for a child is another unknown.

It's hard to imagine that the occasion of my adoption was not a momentous one for the McCutcheons. To arrive home with a walking and talking child must have been a huge moment. Did they have a party? Did they take photographs? Other adoptive parents from that generation talk about the stigma of not being able to have their own children; for them adoption was a secretive affair. Did Mac and Mary hide the fact of my adoption from me in self-protection? Did they reason that if the child does not know then the secret can not get out? I doubt that was the case with me, since the adoption was known about outside the family circle — it was the details of the circumstances that were not. In fact, it appears that the McCutcheons told different stories to different people.

There is one other possibility. When, by whatever means, Mac and Mary came across this little red-haired, freckle-faced boy who was destined to be parentless, they fell in love with him. Two years-plus, cute as a button, walking and talking — an instant child. My childhood friend Jane tells me that her mother had been told a story very close to this by Mary McCutcheon. According to Jane, Mary had gone to an orphanage in the beachside suburb of Sumner. Inside she saw a little two-year-old boy, dressed in pyjamas, standing up in a cot and looking like he needed to be loved. It must have seemed like the easiest thing in the world to take him home.

However, they so much wanted me to be *their* child that they changed the name I already responded to. This was something I obviously couldn't accept, and my subsequent rebellion must have hit them hard. Perhaps they began to question what they'd done. Perhaps they concluded that it was my lower-class genes coming out. Or that my behaviour was a result of something they had failed to do. If that was the case, then their anger towards me could well have been a displacement of guilt.

To date I have been unable to find a record of any orphanage having existed in Sumner, the suburb where Jack – my friend from the old 77 Club days – and Sandra once lived. There is certainly no orphanage there now.

But perhaps the happiest part of my whole story is that I am at last able to say that this knowledge is no longer the most important thing. I now know my real name, and I know my brother, half-brothers and sister. They are enough.

And the other positives in this story? For so much of my life my background was a blank screen on which I could project whatever fantasy I desired. Nothing was real and therefore everything was possible. This was one up side of my situation. It was rich with potential, and whenever I embraced something it usually became an exhaustive – some might say obsessive – journey of discovery. My early forays into literature, in which I consumed my parents' library, left me wearing glasses but in love with the beauty of language.

The research skills I began to develop at that time have stood me in good stead all my life. The search for my roots gave me a far wider exposure to places and people than many of my New Zealand contemporaries. It certainly contributed to my view of the world.

My immersion in Jewish culture gave me a sense of what tribal and family ties could mean. I owe my Jewish friends a debt of gratitude for the times when, although perplexed by my hunger for connection, they welcomed me into their homes and their lives. With such simple acts as lighting *Shabbat* candles, for example, came an instant bond with an ancient heritage that centred around the one thing I craved – family. While I have a deep disquiet about Israel's behaviour towards the Palestinians, I have been enriched by my close encounter with Judaism. And by Yiddish literature, particularly such writers as Shalom Aleichem and his son Shalom Asch (1880–1957), who wrote, 'Now, more than any time previous in human history, we must arm ourselves with an ethical code so that each of us will be aware that he is protecting the moral merchandise absent of which life is not worth living.' Other writers, like Isaac Bashevis Singer, opened up for me the world of Jewish fantasy and a love of the supernatural.

On the opposite side of the emotional spectrum was the profound effect on me of the Shoah. When I was a teenager the stories of the holocaust gave me nightmares, not solely because of the scope of the tragedy, but because I identified so strongly with the children who survived. To have endured that terror only to emerge parentless or, as happened in many cases, without family of any kind, struck me as an obscenely cruel fate. Yet time and again I read accounts by people who, despite what they had been through, had retained their faith. Theirs was a horror that gave perspective to my own situation. Compared to that hell my case was insignificant. Over the years I drew on this to claw myself out of depression; I reminded myself how lucky I was.

There's been another by-product of my teenage fascination with the nightmare of the holocaust and that is an abiding belief that the transition from civilised behaviour to barbarism is often insidious and incremental. It is confirmed by Shalom Asch's plea for a personal set of ethics. Yet ethics come at a cost. If one is not to shuffle mindlessly towards Auschwitz, one has to step off the treadmill early. This is not an easy task, as any whistleblower will be quick to assert. To stand firm against injustice, be it America's war in Vietnam, the treatment of indigenous peoples, the destruction of natural heritage, exacts a price.

At times that cost is personal, as it was for me in the break-up of my first marriage; at others it impacts on professional life. This was the case for me in the divisive debate over the illegal war in Iraq and the plight of asylum seekers. Taking an ethical stand in direct opposition to the policies of Australia's mainstream political parties while being an employee of the national broadcaster has sometimes been problematic. If I were a doctor or a farmer it would perhaps be less of a issue, and I have in instances resorted to self-censorship, which is again insidious, and also soul-destroying. Being even-handed and unbiased is one thing, but to have to sit on your hands while so many lies and distortions are pedalled by politicians and a generally unquestioning media has filled me with self-disgust.

I have been nagged by the question of where to draw the line. When is an issue worth going to the wall for? Many commentators have drawn parallels with 1930s Europe, and the world knows only too well the cost exacted by the failure of people to speak up then. Yet I know that nothing can be gained by speaking out in such a way that could lead to my program being cancelled – it offers too rare an opportunity for public debate to be put in jeopardy. After much reflection, I have come to see that I must keep quiet on air and make my feelings known by other avenues. Nevertheless it is at times an uncomfortable compromise.

One aspect in particular of the drift towards the extreme right in Australian politics stirs up the past for me. My reaction to the incarceration of any refugee is the same as most thinking Australians – one of anger and disgust – but my anger and my disgust is even stronger when there are children involved. Such abuse reaches to the core of my being. I see the child behind the razor wire and I have a physical reaction that is directly linked to my own childhood experience of abandonment. Watching a normally decent nation like Australia being manipulated one step at a time to the point where the majority do not care enough to protest has shocked me deeply. This is not to ignore the thousands of men and women of conscience who have been fighting this national disgrace since its beginnings under the Labor Party. But it's a dark irony that those who have protested have been branded 'un-Australian' for doing so.

The end of the road that Australia has embarked on with its isolated detention centres and its response to the *Tampa* is not, of course, Auschwitz, but those Australians who did not raise their voices then helped pave the way to Guantanamo, the Iraq War and the sanctioned torture at Abu Ghraib. I take solace in the fact that New Zealand has held to a moral position and in doing so has been heralded around the world. I have no doubt that Australians will look back at the lies and deceit they have allowed their government to perpetrate during this period with profound regret. Sadly, that will not heal those who have been killed or injured or denied refuge.

If my reaction to these kinds of events is in part due to sensitivity stemming from the events of my childhood, then I would have it no other way. All religious trappings can fall away as long as there is compassion. In some small measure my politics comes from my blood. I felt my childhood as a great injustice and now injustice touches my heart.

Another positive legacy of my background is my curiosity

about the world and everything in it, a direct result of searching for my roots. Those journeys to Europe, the weeks and months spent watching and listening, desperate for a clue to my origins, were not wasted, fruitless though they felt at the time. I channelled my curiosity into writing. All the places and characters I encountered along the way are a gift, a privilege – they fire my imagination and inhabit the pages of my novels.

My pattern of behaviour in intimate relationships has also changed dramatically. For years my deep-seated belief that I was not worthy of affection caused me to create the conditions where this belief would be fulfilled. I undermined my relationships, sabotaging them so that they conformed to my view of the world. Being abandoned, my subconscious convinced me, was my destiny.

Naturally this proved disastrous for those I was involved with and caused a great deal of unhappiness. Even the concept of home felt like something I was not worthy of having. My desire to belong was diametrically opposed by my behaviour, whereby I set out to prove I was a failure.

This state of mind was the first thing to drop away after discovering my real family, and the living proof of it is my relationship with my brother and sister. Suddenly the self-confidence that had always been a facade was real. It's no coincidence that I married again only six months after our family reunion, and that Suzanna and I have a wonderful relationship, far beyond anything I had previously thought possible.

While the journey from disturbed child to content adult has been long and difficult, it has given me much with which to approach the next stage of my life. I am forever indebted to the friends who have stood by me and put up with my sudden changes of direction.

Every Sunday evening for the past few years an extraordinary group of people have gathered at my house for a sauna. They are an eclectic bunch who span the employment alphabet from ambulance officer to zoologist. In between are musicians, writers, electricians and actors, giving the gathering the feeling of an old-fashioned soirée. After a sauna and a swim, we share a meal and round the evening out with contributions from the artists. Refreshed in body and spirit, we're in the perfect state to begin a new week. To have such friends is a blessing that has enriched my life beyond measure.

Postscript

The universe does not take heed of publishing schedules when delivering life's major surprises. Late in December 2004, just as this manuscript was due to go to the typesetter, I woke one morning at five a.m. with the conviction – absolutely clear but for no reason that I could name – that I must check my email. I got out of bed, put some coffee on to brew and booted up the laptop.

Awaiting me were two emails from the same person. The sender was unknown to me, and for a moment I thought they might be spam. I clicked on the one that had been sent first.

To: Sandy@McCutcheon.com
Date: Tue, 21 Dec 2004 18:29:36
Subject: Trying to contact Robert/Sandy McCutcheon

Dear Sandy/Robert,

This may appear to be a strange request, but I am attempting to contact a person named Robert McCutcheon whose nickname is Sandy. He is from New Zealand, Christchurch we think. He studied Journalism and was in the UK in the late 60s (66–67?). It was there he met an Irish woman training to be a nurse named Margaret (Peig) Cleary. Before Sandy left the UK, he and Margaret went to Scotland for a visit with friends.

If you can help or have the time to reply, either way, I would greatly appreciate it. My name is Yvonne Duane, I live in Dublin, Ireland and my phone number is . . .

I hope to hear from you soon.

Yours sincerely, Yvonne Duane

Suddenly I was wide awake but greatly confused. Margaret Cleary was the Irish woman who had written to me back in the 1960s saying she'd had a child by me, whom she'd named Chantelle Noelle. So who was this Yvonne? The second email left me in no doubt.

To: Sandy@McCutcheon.com
Date: Tue, 21 Dec 2004 14:52:59
Subject: From your website – trying to contact Robert (Sandy McCutcheon)

Dear Sandy,

I don't know if I have the right person, I'm looking for a man called Robert McCutcheon, nickname Sandy, who was in the UK in 1966–67 and who knew a woman called Margaret (Peig) Cleary – an Irish woman. If you are that person I would very much like to set up contact, have a conversation or two. I am the birth daughter of Margaret and was given up for adoption. I traced and found Margaret 2 years ago. My name is Yvonne Duane, and I am now 36, I live in Dublin and have two children.

Please reply if you can.

Thanks, Yvonne

My immediate response was one of absolute joy and amazement. Maha had long been teasing me about her Irish sister, and whenever I told people I had four children she would correct me and say it was five. Over the years, I'd developed a habit of asking every Irish person I met if they'd ever come across a Chantelle Cleary, and in the 1980s and 1990s I searched the Irish genealogical databases for her name, to no effect. And now here she was, my long-lost fifth child.

I could barely take it all in. Nevertheless within minutes I was calling Dublin, then speaking with Yvonne. Just like that. After thirty-six years.

The relief at having finally traced me was evident in her

voice and we talked for a long time, until she had to go and put her children to bed. That done, she phoned back and we resumed our conversation. The story I heard of her adoption and subsequent search for her family bore uncanny parallels with my own.

Yvonne had been adopted by a good couple who were given no information about her by the adoption agency, other than the comment that 'one of her parents was probably French, as she had originally been given a French name'. In acknowledgement of this European connection, her new parents called her Yvonne. They were open with her from the start about her adoption, but could provide no accurate details about her birth.

As a teenager Yvonne set out to discover her real parents, but time and again she was blocked by bureaucrats who told her it was unlikely records had been kept. Then came a breakthrough. She received a letter from a nun/social worker in the agency that had handled her adoption, informing her that her mother's name was Margaret, and her father's Robert. He was a New Zealander and had made several attempts to persuade Margaret to take her child to New Zealand to live. The knowledge that she *had* been wanted by her natural father was a balm to Yvonne, and she kept the nun's letter with her throughout her early twenties, reading it again and again.

This initial breakthrough was followed by years of frustration. Yvonne discovered that there were files on her case after all, but she was repeatedly told by the bureaucrats that they were 'under no obligation to do tracing' for her. Her anger at this response was still evident as she recounted the story to me, and I was grateful for it, because it was this anger that had fuelled her persistence in finding the truth.

Nothing further happened until 2002, when Yvonne was finally allocated a case worker, ten years after her initial request for one. The case worker made contact with Yvonne's mother, and learned she was willing to meet her daughter. Letters were exchanged, and eventually the two met in what seems to me a bizarre choice of venue: the Dolmen Hotel in Carlow, County Wexford, exactly the same hotel where Margaret had been coerced into giving Yvonne up some thirty-four years earlier.

Margaret's story was a sad one. Returning pregnant and single to Ireland, she was pressured by her family and local clergy to give her baby up for adoption. She resisted, and when she gave birth on 6 January 1968 in a mothers-and-babies hostel she attempted to smuggle her daughter away by climbing out a window the night before she was due to hand her over to the authorities. But she was caught and the adoption went ahead.

When the two of them were reunited Margaret confirmed what Yvonne had been told by the nun years earlier – that I had offered to bring them both to New Zealand to live. But at the time, Margaret had felt this was not the right thing to do. She also passed on the important detail that Robert

McCutcheon's nickname was Sandy.

Armed with this information, Yvonne set out to track me down. Life got in the way for a while, with marriage, a doctorate in clinical psychology, and the birth of her two children all demanding her attention. When she returned to the case in December 2004 it was simply a matter of a Google search and she had my email address.

She fired off an email, but when her husband read what she'd written he thought it a bit 'chaotic'. Excited and not thinking straight, Yvonne sent a second, more formal email saying basically the same thing. When I phoned, some three hours after her first email, her husband answered. He handed her the phone saying casually, 'Yvonne, it's Sandy for you.' She'd assumed he was joking and was incredulous to find her father on the line.

During our hours of phone conversations I learned that Yvonne was planning to spend Christmas in her hometown of Cashel, in County Tipperary. In another strange coincidence, this was a place much loved by Suzanna and me. We had spent time there just two years before, and the Rock of Cashel was our favourite spot in Ireland. Now I learned from Yvonne that the area around the old ruins of the rock had been her childhood playground. When I mentioned that Suzanna and I were travelling after Christmas to the Moroccan city of Fès, where we were in the process of buying a house, it took just twenty-four hours for Yvonne to decide to meet us there, along with her husband and children.

I could hardly contain my emotions. Being found by Yvonne was just wonderful, certainly the best Christmas present imaginable, but I was unsure how I felt about being an instant grandfather. Under normal circumstances, becoming a grandparent was an evolving process, like becoming a parent, and yet I had been one for two-and-a-half years without knowing. It would take a little getting used to.

Due to differing work commitments, Suzanna and I travelled separately to Morocco and I arrived in Fès ahead of her on 6 January, to find that eight months of complex negotiations had failed to nail down the purchase of the house we'd chosen. In order to complete the transaction, the current owners needed all the members of their family to sign a clearance. They discovered in the process that their own purchase of the house had not been completed properly, and that an important document existed only as a photocopy where the law insisted on the original. That was tough because the signatory to the document had since died. It was explained to me that a court document could be obtained to clear the path for a sale but that it might take months, or even years. It seemed clear that I needed a plan-B.

On our previous trip a year earlier, I ran out of time and had to return to Australia, leaving Suzanna to do the house-hunting. She had eventually found a traditional riad-style dwelling in the World Heritage-listed medina, after spending a couple of weeks looking at eight or more houses a day. The likelihood of my finding something suitable before Yvonne and her family arrived on 14 January seemed impossible.

Nevertheless I threw myself into the task and struck gold the first day: a 300-year-old riad built around a beautiful courtyard with orange and lemon trees, and with ancient mosaic tiles throughout. It had carved cedar ceilings, stained-glass windows, and a million-dollar view of both medina and mountains from the third-floor terraces. An engineer's report gave the place a clean bill of health and the old couple who owned it were eager to sell. Most importantly, they had all the paperwork in order. We shook hands on an in-principle agreement, and all that was needed was for Suzanna to arrive, like the house and we had a deal.

None of this frantic activity managed to dispel my rising fear that something would go wrong and Yvonne would cancel her trip. I fell back into my old habits and every possible disaster scenario got a run in my over-anxious mind. We would be incompatible. She and the children would hate Fès. Her husband would think the entire trip a waste of time and money. Spending a week together seemed like a situation fraught with risks.

By the time 14 January arrived I was a nervous wreck. As their flight was not due in until evening, I prepared a bag of bread, fruit, yoghurt, cheese and biscuits for their room so the children would have something to eat on arrival. That took all of ten minutes and I spent the remainder of the day walking the lanes and alleyways of the medina, trying to stay in front of my fears. By the time I was in a taxi to the airport I was feeling physically ill. To my surprise the taxi was not involved in a crash and suddenly I was in the arrivals hall, watching people coming through customs.

It was all eerily reminiscent of waiting at Brisbane airport for Bronwen and Glyn: my life had turned into *Goundhog Day*. Just as I had in Brisbane, I eyed every woman who came through customs, wondering if they were Yvonne. Any woman with two children in tow who walked towards me was potentially her, and it was to my relief that the more grim-faced of them kept going. The flow of people eventually became a trickle and then – nothing. My worst fears had been realised. Yvonne had got cold feet and called the trip off. Whoever was directing this movie was a sadist.

Then I noticed movement in the customs hall and a woman appeared with two children and two adults. There could be no mistaking my daughter. Ignoring the barriers and security guards, I went straight to her. For an instant we looked at each other. There should have been some cool first remark, some notable first line, but neither of us was capable of speaking. The sickness I had been feeling vanished in a hug and I remember blinking through tears and mumbling something inane like, 'I don't know what to say.'

Yvonne's husband, Mark Siung, a filmmaker, editor and

writer, was quite unfazed. He grinned and greeted me warmly. His sister Jenny, who had come along at the last moment to provide babysitting support so that Yvonne and I could spend more time together, looked delighted by the whole thing. Little Nisha and Nathan, however, were exhausted and in need of food and bed, so we bundled ourselves into a taxi and headed back to Fès.

Later, with the children tucked up in bed, Yvonne and I found time to sit quietly on our own. She had brought a number of childhood photographs to show me and I was amazed at how like Maha she looked as a child – they were so alike as to be spooky.

To my delight and considerable relief, the next few days were fantastically easy. Yvonne, Mark, Jenny, Nisha and Nathan all fell in love with Fès and, unlike many foreigners, were not intimidated by the medina's spiderweb of lanes and alleyways – more than nine and a half thousand in all. They were soon ranging far and wide, picking up enough street Arabic to order coffee and greet and thank people. I was impressed. Stepping into the Fès medina is akin to stepping back several hundred years in time, and the effect can be overpowering. But there was nowhere my suddenly expanded family would not go.

On the day I organised for a guide to show them some of the medina's hard-to-find treasures, Mark must have set some sort of record for taking a stroller through the centuries-old cobbled streets and stairways. Yvonne gave the riad I was proposing to buy the thumbs-up and declared it perfect for future family holidays.

The next day Suzanna arrived and also declared the house suitable. She and Yvonne liked each other from the first moment, and Suzanna took to the role of step-grandmother with an ease that astounded me.

My granddaughter Nisha, at two-and-a-half, apparently had a reputation for being shy but I was soon 'her Sandy'. With her, along with one-year-old Nathan, I was discovering how rewarding being a grandparent can be. Beneath the surface, though, a lot was going on for Yvonne and me. My emotional release at having made contact produced a sudden bout of sickness, the severity of which I had only experienced once before in my life, on the night in Akaroa when I discovered my real name. A fever now hit me so hard that on the third night I collapsed on the floor of my hotel room with vivid hallucinations. Suzanna had the presence of mind to douse me with cold water and I recovered quickly, but I developed a nagging cough.

For her part, Yvonne was going back to her room every night and bursting into tears, crying with sheer relief. But amid all this emotional turmoil we found time each day to sit and swap stories of searching for our parents.

Yvonne had been fortunate in having adoptive parents who were up front with her about her adoption, but they'd been as much in the dark about her birth parents as she was. And so Yvonne, with an imagination as fertile as my own, fantasised about her French father, picturing him as a traveller leading an exciting life before being cruelly parted from her mother.

Our imaginations weren't the only thing my daughter and I had in common. The more time we spent together, the more we were convinced by the case for nature in the nature-versus-nurture debate. The similarities between us were extraordinary, too strong to be mere coincidence. As I said to Yvonne, if I had set out to conjure a daughter who encapsulated all the values I hold to, I could not have improved on her. Her sense of justice and compassion, her philosophical beliefs and her sense of humour were all a perfect fit.

Around us the universe fell into place. The house sale went through without a hitch, although the mediaeval method of transaction was a surprise. There were no lawyers, just scribes who unrolled a scroll bearing the names of all those who had owned the dwelling over the centuries. The old woman who was selling the place put her thumbprint for a signature, and Suzanna and I unloaded our pockets of huge stacks of dirhams to pay in cash.

The sale was celebrated by a glass of flavoured milk and some home-baked cookies. Down in the courtyard, sheep were tethered to the lemon tree in readiness for sacrifice the following day, during the festival of l'Aid Al Adha. I tried not to think of the blood on what were now Suzanna's and my tiles.

I was due to leave Fès the day after the sale, all too soon. Saying farewell to Yvonne and her family was inevitably difficult, but at least we had established the basis for a developing relationship, and we had a house in which to share holidays, one that didn't involve the children in a 24-hour plane trip. I must have still been holding a lot of pent-up emotion, because after taking off from Casablanca I found myself unable to stop crying. So many conflicting – yet all too familiar – feelings tumbled out. Grief at the years robbed from both of us. Joy at the pleasure of Yvonne's company. And sadness at the thought of how long it might be before we got to sit down together again. When the sadness lifted, though, I was left with a warm glow and a smile on my face. I was blessed with another incredible daughter and friend.

Were my life story a work of fiction, an editor would have put a pen through this postscript, citing lack of credibility. I would have agreed. But sometimes life brings miracles, and this one was pure magic.

Afterword

by Bronwen Watson

I finished reading a draft of Sandy's life story today. We are more alike than I would have believed. He remembers his childhood in the same way I do – as images from an old movie, except that many of his memories really did come from old movies. I found that this way of looking at the past made a lot of events less personal, and therefore less painful.

There are concrete similarities too. Sandy writes, 'Everything was ordered, neat and in the correct place.' When we lived with Irene our house was neat and tidy too, and nothing was ever out of place. Open any cupboard or drawer at any time and everything would be placed with military precision.

And we both had ritual in our early lives; Glyn and I were up at six each day, and the house was ready for Irene's inspection by eight. We had to be home from school by four every afternoon or punishment would be meted out. No excuse was accepted. Regrettably there was no comforting warmth of a Mrs Parsons for us at the end of the day.

But that's where the comparison ends. Sandy's description of life in the 1950s is alien to me. We never went into department stores where the staff knew our name. We went to whichever school was closest and usually never stayed at one long enough to become known, even to our classmates. Not long ago I was surfing the Web, looking for one of the many schools I attended. They were planning a reunion and were asking old students to register interest. I was tempted to do so, but then I realised that no one would remember who I was.

For a long time cruelty and violence were part of everyday life for me, not just a subject that was discussed over supper as it was in Sandy's family. I accepted the abuse I received from Irene as normal. Morris might not have been aware of just how serious the situation had become, as I never dared say anything to him. I had been warned by Irene of the consequences of telling him what went on when he was away. Of course he must have felt the tension, but what could he do?

I remember the day I heard about Sandy – 29 October 1998 – as a hot and steamy day with thunderstorms off and on all afternoon. My husband was impatient to get to his club for a meeting and was not happy when I stopped to answer the phone. As soon as I heard Glyn's voice I knew there was a problem. He only called if there was bad news.

At the time I didn't comprehend what he was telling me; I had no idea who this Brian he was talking about was. As far as I was concerned, our younger brother's name was Barry. Our mother had called him by that name when I visited her in the 1950s. I remember asking her where my brother was and she told me 'Barry' was at school, and then she asked me to say that I was her sister if any of the neighbours called. Joan must have misunderstood who I was asking after, and I didn't know then that she had two other sons – Barry and Philip, my half-brothers – and so the name stuck in my memory.

I later found out that Norm had told Joan not to have any contact with Glyn or me, and my mother was no doubt more concerned about Norm not learning of my visit than she was with answering any questions I had, or bringing me up to date with my new half-brothers.

But now Glyn was insistent about this brother Brian, so I wrote down the number and promised to phone. There had to be a catch, I thought; no matter what this guy called himself, he couldn't be our brother. Maybe he'd looked up 'Parry' in the phone book – B Parry could have been Bert, Brian, Barry, or a host of others. The surname McCutcheon was familiar too, and I wasn't about to be caught in some sort of scam.

The name nagged at me and then it hit me like a bolt of lightning. The host of a talkback program I listened to was called Sandy McCutcheon. The situation was becoming more ludicrous by the minute.

Then there was the fact that my youngest brother, so I thought, had stayed with our mother; he hadn't been adopted. If this man was who he said he was I had to process this new information before I was able to speak to him. All my life I'd believed that the baby of the family had been our mother's favourite. Now I had to come to terms with the fact that she had not wanted any of us.

The next day I had plenty of reasons to delay contacting the man Glyn had spoken to. I had to be at work at the aged-care hostel by six a.m. and had promised to take one of our residents shopping. When I got back home I made coffee and wandered around the house, putting off making the call. I was always good at avoiding contact with strangers – it was something I shunned whenever possible.

When I finally met Sandy I felt in awe of this person who was my brother. He had far more in common with Glyn than with me, and I expected to be pushed aside as they got to know each other better. They could communicate daily via email, while in the beginning I had to rely on the phone and letters. It was embarrassing to admit to Sandy that I couldn't use a computer, when he took it for granted that I could.

Once I got over the initial shock of Sandy being my brother, I wanted to know every little detail about him. I bought his books and read them not once but several times, trying to get into his head. Like Sandy, I have a passion for the written word. He writes them and I read them.

I had trouble explaining the person I was to Sandy back in 1998. I avoided people and I was not very articulate. I had a habit of masking my real feelings by being flippant. It was far easier to joke about the onerous events of the past, and this might have made me seem shallow and flighty when I'm actually the opposite of that.

Through all the excitement of meeting Sandy, I began to see another side to Glyn. We had not been very close during our adult life; I guess we were a reminder to each other of a time we both preferred to forget. With Sandy's appearance it was as if Glyn became another person, a very serious, almost unknowable person. Sadly, once the euphoria of the reunion wore off, Glyn retreated back into isolation again and we only have occasional contact.

Glyn and I are not the ones who were adopted, but when I listen to Sandy tell of his life I think this might have been the better option. Anything would have been better than the life we endured. Sandy missed out on knowing his father, a most caring and loving man. Morris embraced children who were not his own with all the love he was capable of. But along the way his own children missed out on a fulfilling and happy childhood.

We also missed out on growing up with our younger

brother. Sandy grew up not knowing that he had a wonderful extended family willing to accept him no matter who or what he became. Yet he proved to have the Parry tenacity; he rose above the adversity of his childhood and became the respected man we know and love today.

Acknowledgements

Many people assisted me in uncovering the past. Chief among them is my sister Bronwen, who has been tireless in tracking down obscure twigs on the branches of our family tree. As well as writing the afterword for this book, she has also written her own account, 'The Fishmonger's Daughter', a brave and honest description of a life that was far from easy. I certainly hope it finds the publisher it deserves.

A great number of people in New Zealand also gave of their time to help me on the quest. Guy and Marianne Hargreaves not only housed and fed me in Christchurch but also put up with the emotional turmoil I experienced on several occasions, and unstintingly gave love and Scotch in equal measure. Libby Hamilton in Rangiora drove me hundreds of kilometres in search of contacts, and along the way found the perfect places to relax with some fly-fishing. My newly found Aunt Lorna was a font of knowledge and a real joy. Gratitude is also due to Carol Harper and Geoff Parry for permission to draw on their research, and to the whole Parry clan who welcomed me so warmly, especially Lesley, Pauline and Dorothy.

In Australia, Arthur and Carol Parry were a source of much

family history, as well as the best bacon-and-egg pies on the planet. Maria Grist kindly provided the photo of the gompa at Illusion Farm. To the fine people at Penguin Australia – thank you for believing in the story. My editor, Meredith Rose, performed miracles in untangling my memories and syntax.

Finally, my thanks to my wife Suzanna, who was there on the day I finally arrived home.